HAMBLE

A Village History

by
Nicolas Robinson

ISBN 0 946184 32 1
July 1987

Published by
Kingfisher Railway Productions
65A The Avenue, Southampton SO1 2TA

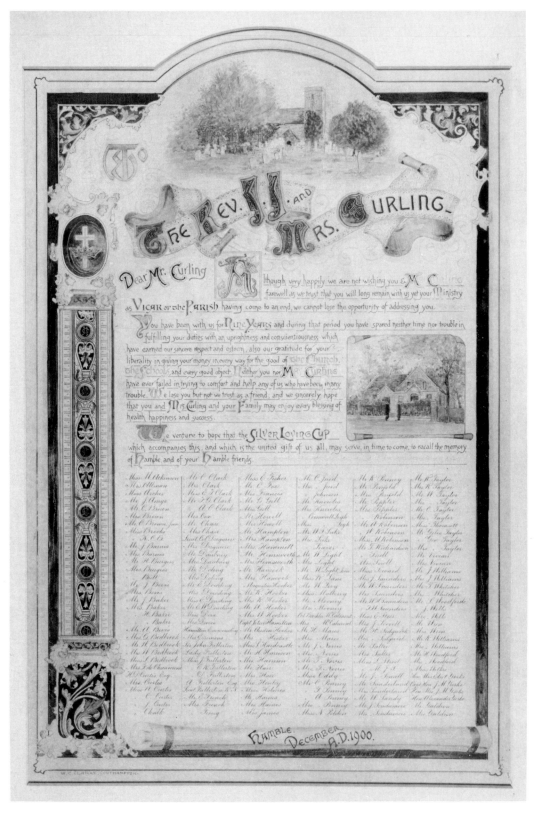

A plaque given by grateful villagers to Joseph James Curling, Vicar of Hamble Church from 1892 to 1900.

Courtesy of Bill Curling

Typeset by Alphaset
65A The Avenue
Southampton
SO1 2TA

Printed by Biddles Ltd.
Guildford
Surrey

Packing fish on the foreshore in 1860. *J. Macpherson*

Loading loam at Badnam Creek, 1920. From a painting by the author's father, Gregory Robinson.

Foreword

It may seem odd to the reader that little has been written about the history of the village of Hamble and the river. Indeed, few of today's residents are aware of the part it has played over the centuries in shipbuilding, trade, the aircraft and oil industries, yachting and many other activities. Establishments such as the College of Air Training and the training ship *Mercury* have played their part and are sadly now no more.

Among those who have had associations with Hamble are C.B. Fry and his cricketing friends W.G. Grace and Ranjitsinhji, Robert van Buren Emmons, the Earls of Hardwicke, Nevil Shute, Admiral Fullerton, Sir Henry Maynwaring, Sir Alan Cobham, Juan de la Cierva, A.V. Roe, H.P. Folland, Basil Lubbock, Sir Robert Baden-Powell, Bert Hinkler and many, many more.

They have all left their mark on Hamble and the village is the richer.

So many members of our Royal Family have visited Hamble for one purpose or another that they are almost too numerous to detail.

The Quay, showing left to right: Leonard House, Sundial Cottage, Magnolia Cottage.

Hamble-Le-Rice

According to the Oxford Dictionary of Place Names, the name is derived from Old English adjective 'hamel' which seems to have meant 'maimed' but very likely originally meant 'crooked'. 'Rice' is Old English meaning 'brushwood'.

Others suggest the name comes from Hamele, a thane of the Saxon Meonwaris.

Throughout the centuries, the spelling has changed considerably and below are some of the variants, with dates when first recorded:-

Hamelea	circa 730	Hamele in the Rys	1401
Hamble	901	Hamull in ye Hoke	1415
Amle	1147	Hamil on the Hoke	1485
Hamele	1320	Hamyll	1485
Hamil Hoke	1345	Hammel	1496
Hamble le Rice	1354	Ambua	1500
Hamelhoke	1355	Hameline	1509
Hamel	1369	Hammell de Ryse	1553

Hamble Howcke	1566	Ham-en-le-Rice	1846
Hambell	1566	Hamblerice	1928
Hamble Ryse	1568	Hamell, Hamull	
Hammble	1576	Hamel Hooke	
Hable	1648	Hamble-Rice	
Hamble	1725	Hamble-en-le-Rys	

The Tithing of Satchell derives its name from Sir Henry Shatershall, a knight of Henry III's day (1216-1272) and was included in the parish of Hamble in 1902.

Shatershall	1216	Shatshan	1676
Shatshole	1566	Sachel	1725
Stratshawe	1570	Sachell	1725
Shatshall	1585	Satchell	1841
Shatshel	1607	Satchel	1894
Shatsham	1648		

Contents

Dedication

Old photographs and pictures, old memories and records are the material of which history is made. To those who have safeguarded such information through the ages, this book is dedicated.

A sketch of the Bugle public house.

The Hamble

The Hamble is an old river geologically speaking: its waters have cut its bed down to sea level for practically its whole length, allowing the salt sea to reach as far as Botley. Beyond Botley Mill there is only a stream. The course of the River has wandered and, as its name implies, is now very 'crooked'.

Throughout the ages, the natural development of settlements has been affected by the local geography and geology and by technical advances. There must be almost as many reasons for the existence of villages or towns as there are such places. In primitive times, man could cross a river only where he could ford it and so we are almost certain to find some early form of habitation at the lowest place on the river where it can be crossed, either on foot or later on horseback; later still, where the river can conveniently be crossed by ferry, that is where there is firm ground on either side; still later, where a bridge can be built. The highest navigable point for seagoing ships will also encourage the foundation of a town.

In other regions, one can expect to find a settlement on a hill top or other place that could have easily been defended in early days or where roads between large communities cross other such roads. Centres of large agricultural areas, too, would give rise to a market town. Small villages tended to mark a day's journey from a large city on foot or on horseback or by coach. Some places owe their existence to the presence of coal, tin, iron or water. Reasons for their growth are legion.

But what of Hamble? In 730 A.D. the Venerable Bede, who travelled the whole country writing his Chronicles, wrote of the place: '. . . two tides out of the Northern Ocean do daily meet and encounter near the mouth of the River Hamelea and when their conflict is ended return again to the sea whence they came.' Even at that time, the peculiarity of the double tides which cause the water to stand for two hours at high water were noted and caused wonder. No doubt the Romans remarked upon it too for they used the Hamble and the Itchen.

Let us look at the tides in more detail: as the earth spins, water is drawn by the moon, causing a small tidal wave. Only in the southern 'Roaring Forties' can this wave pass right round the world, which it does once every twenty-four hours or so: 19,000 miles at a speed of about 750 miles an hour. From this 'mother' tide, waves are sent speeding up the various oceans, slowing down as they get into shallower water and steepening. It is probably three and a half days before the mother wave reaches the Hamble but, by now, it has slowed down, taking twelve hours to reach Dover, a further 130 miles, at only 11 miles an hour.

Aerial view of the river 1930

Added to this, of course, there is the complication of the moon's effect on the waters in the Northern Hemisphere. The height of the wave at Hamble is about 14 feet and, from the crest, the tidal stream runs eastward up the Channel on the flood and, as the crest passes, the stream runs off the back of the wave to the west in the Channel as well as in the Solent. As this is taking place, the water, endeavouring to run out of Southampton Water and the Hamble River, is held up by the west-going stream for about two hours. This means that Southampton and Hamble have slack water at high tide twice a day.

This phenomenon is invaluable for docking vessels today, just as it has been throughout the centuries of sailing ships. More than for any other reason it is this to which the settlements on the banks of the Hamble River owe their existence.

By its geographical position, the River was destined to become a centre for shipping and other factors were to dictate the type of ships which used the haven.

The two hours of slack water have the effect of delaying the ebb which is consequently stronger once it starts and so has a greater scouring effect to keep the channel from silting up. The slack allows silt to settle and this remains on the banks. It is noticeable that there is no mud in places where there is little or no influx of fresh water. Although the watershed or catchment area of the River Hamble is not large, a considerable quantity of fresh water finds its way into the estuary, bringing with it many particles held in colloidal suspension until it mixes with salt water. Then, due to chemical reaction, the particles run together, forming larger particles which settle to the bottom. This silting is increased by slack water and Hamble Mud has been a comfortable resting place for centuries for ships which are laid up. The mud is very fine and gribble and other pests can live only in the top few inches. Below that the mud, by keeping out the air, acts as

a preservatives and the timbers of old ships are still sound after hundreds of years.

The mud is very deep in places and there are only occasional spits of firm ground reaching below high water mark and so it has been difficult to build many houses jutting into the water. The shipbuilding industry of the 17th and 18th centuries made use of the few firm expanses of the shoreline. The ships were built in the open, as close to the water as possible.

There is part of a confined aquifer passing under Hamble and this has been tapped in the grounds of the College of Air Training. This is sometimes referred to by laymen as an underground river and is a few hundred feet below ground. It is, however, not the sort of river we find on the surface but a seam of gravel, possibly some former beach long since buried, through which water can find its way with relative ease. Over this seam is an impermeable layer and, when this is drilled through, the water below is forced up to within about 50 feet of the surface.

Of the rainfall, about one-third immediately runs off to the sea as surface water, a third is lost by evaporation, either directly or through plant life, and the remaining third soaks into the ground, some of this coming to light in the form of springs.

There was one such spring with clear fresh water at the foot of the bank between the Oyster and Ferry Hards and another at Westfield Common on the beach. This latter, Caddick Well, was used to water vessels which anchored offshore. Bottles of this water were sent as far afield as Surrey for its holy or medicinal quality. One old man told how, as a boy, he had been sent to fill a bottle to send away but dropped it on the way home and refilled it at the duck pond in Hamble Lane. He chuckled as he wondered how the recipient liked it!

This spring, once regarded as a 'holy well', is now in a sad state of neglect but used to bear the inscription, 'Let him that

Well and Pump in Well Lane, closed 1909.

thirsteth drink of this water' on its surrounding stonework which was erected by the Yorke family. It had been used at least since Elizabethan times to fill the fresh water casks of vessels anchored off in Netley Roads and later by the Southampton Pilots' ketches.

Drinking water was found in the many wells in the village. There was one behind Sundial Cottage on the Quay, one on *Taylor's Wharf and a public one in Well Lane at the back of †Copperhill Terrace. There is still a pump behind Mr. Taylor's house in the High Street with a lead lining, dated 1804, and another at Pump Cottage. The public one in Well Lane was condemned by the Health Authorities in 1909 as it had become polluted by sewerage. Fresh water in plenty could be taken in Satchell Lane near the Mercury until recent developments. There were wells at the Victory Inn and the Olde House, a pump at Manor Cottages and a pump and well at Manor Farm. A pump, too, was in a field by Beaulieu Road for watering the cattle. The provision of fresh water in Hamble has never been a problem.

So, up to a certain size of vessel, we have ideal conditions for the development of shipping and shipbuilding. Its double tides; its twisting course which deterred invaders, Saxon, Jutish and French; the ease with which it could be defended; fresh water for inhabitants and vessels alike; mud berths for all who needed them; and plenty of timber for building within easy reach. In 1720, Daniel Defoe wrote: 'Here is a building yard for ships of war . . . it seems the safety of the creek and the plenty of timber in the country behind it is the reason for building so much here'.

Caddick well on Westfield Common.

* Taylor's Wharf was owned by the Taylor family, builders, undertakers and coal merchants since 1800. They lived in a Georgian house in the High Street. The last Taylor, Alfred, died in 1973, aged 78, his father, Charles, in 1962, aged 97, after more than 70 years of marriage.

† Well Lane, formerly Copperhill, so named because it was the location of coppers for boiling tar used for the preservation of rope, etc.

Yachts in mudberths at Lukes' Yard.

Aerial view of Fairey Marine and the River at Hamble Point.

River Banks

The banks of the Hamble River, and indeed those of most creeks in the area, were held in place by rice grass, as it was known locally. This was the small, tough Spartina Stricta which grew extensively, consolidating the mud banks. About 1870, Spartina Alterniflora made its appearance. This was a larger plant but not so robust and probably came from Canada or the U.S. and may have been in a vessel which sank off Lymington or spilled at Eling where grasses from the 'New World' were imported as well as Stipa Tenacissima, a native of North Africa, for paper making. It is also said that it came from palliasses emptied by troops returning to Southampton by ship.

The present grass is Spartina Townsendii and is a cross, being larger and stronger than the original, and has obliterated Spartina Stricta, none of which is now found in the district. It was, however, found to be unsuitable for paper making because of difficulties in bleaching but it has been re-planted in various parts of the country to reclaim land or hold mudbanks in place, though it needs to be replaced after about 30 years by other

grasses. It is unfortunately easily killed by oil spillage and the once extensive area on Hamble Spit by Faireys has almost completely disappeared and, as the roots rot, the mud is washed away. Until the last war, there was a large bed of rice grass where dinghies are now kept on the Hard.

The distinction between Saltings and Salterns is not today always appreciated. Saltings are the lands covered by salt water at high tide, whereas Salterns were shallow salt pans where sea water was allowed to flood in and was left to evaporate in the sun. As it evaporated, more salt water might be allowed in and the resulting brine was then boiled, leaving the salt. A wet summer which kept adding fresh rain-water meant disaster but in some places this method of obtaining salt was continued into the 1870s.

During William III's reign (1689-1702), the Government imposed a tax on salt which by 1805 had risen to fifteen shillings (75p) per bushel. The tax was abolished in 1824.

Hamble had a Salt Officer who lived in a house at the Salterns on Hamble Point.

Across the River, showing Lukes' original boatyard and the Salt Officer's house, about 1905.

Past History

It can be seen then that, geographically, the Hamble area has many advantages, having fertile soil and fresh water, forests of oak and, no doubt, plenty of wild life in them. Neolithic man (6000 – 1700 B.C.) left in Hamble some of his stone implements – they were dug up in a gravel pit in Satchell Lane. There is an ancient barrow on Hamble Common (date unknown) and there is evidence of Roman occupation: broken Roman pottery was discovered in the 1920s by Badnam Creek and a find in 1968 on the Recreation Ground of over two and a half thousand bronze Roman coins is further evidence of early habitation.

These coins had been in an earthenware jar, which unfortunately was broken, and date from about 320 A.D., most being minted for Constantine the Great or for his three sons, but in the collection there were coins of several other Caesars of about the same date.

Constantine I became Caesar of Britain in 306 A.D. He built Constantinople (now Istanbul), was the first Roman Emperor to turn Christian and gave religious freedom in 314 to the Christians who had been persecuted until that time. He brought many good reforms, including right of appeal and abolition of imprisonment without trial and remained in power for 31 years. During his supremacy, trade within the Roman Empire was able to flourish and it is not surprising that coins from nearly all over his domain were found in the Hamble collection.

The coins bear no date: this can be ascertained from the head of the Caesar on the obverse and, as most were in power for only a year or two, this is reasonably accurate. On the reverse, or the exergue (the part occupied by the date on more modern coins) is shown the mark of the place where the coin was minted. Among the first hundred Hamble coins to be catalogued are some from Trier (in the Moselle valley), Arelate (Arles, Southern France), Lugdunum (Lyons), Salonica (in Greece), Roma, Aquileia (Italian-Jugoslav border), Siscia (Jugoslavia), Nicomedia (Turkey), Heraclea (near Istanbul) and Antioch (Syria). That coins so varied and from so far afield should end up in one collection in Hamble leads one to believe that the Hamble was used as a port of entry and to speculate as to what type of trade was being carried on.

In 410 A.D. the Roman legions were withdrawn and Britain was left without an army to repel invaders. The Norsemen or Normans from Scandinavia invaded and settled in Northern France on either side of the Seine. Saxons from Saxony, Angles from Southern Denmark, Danes from the Danish Islands and Southern Sweden and Jutes from Northern Denmark (Jutland) invaded Britain.

Roman coin. One of many unearthed at Hamble.

Corner of High Street, 1905.

The approach to the village, High Street 1905.

Looking down the High Street towards the Square.

Hamble, Hants

The Square, about 1905. The Olde House is on the right.

The Gun House and School Lane 1905.

Thatched Cottages, Satchell Lane, Daffodil Terrace right.

Before 550 A.D. the Jutes were in possession of the Isle of Wight and the area between Southampton and Portsmouth. About 730 A.D. the chronicler Bede wrote of Hamble as being in the land of the Jutes and remarked upon its tides.

They erected on the Common a promontory fortress, still clearly visible. Behind this they could retire when hard pressed and break out to plunder the surrounding countryside at will. There are small earthworks within the fortress. Before long, however, the area was taken over by the West Saxons and incorporated in Wessex.

Pilgrimages to the Holy Land may be said to have been started by St. Helena, the mother of Constantine, who is alleged to have discovered the True Cross in 326 A.D. In 722 St. Willebald, a West Saxon, and his companions decided 'to reach and gaze upon the walls of that delectable and desirable city of Jerusalem' and set off from Hamble. They were imprisoned 'as strangers and unknown men' in Syria but were released by Yezid II when he learned they were 'from the western shore, where the sun sets, and we know not of any land beyond – nothing but sea'.

It was King Alfred who first attempted to repel the Danish invaders by meeting them at sea and there is strong evidence that two Danish ships ran aground in the Hamble estuary and, when the tide ebbed, their crews were slain.

The Saxons were largely farmers and not like the warlike and better organized Normans who invaded in 1066 from across the Channel, bringing with them the feudalism they had learnt from the French. The Normans were Christians and were soon in command in Wessex.

Edward III, in his attempt to gain the crown of France, fought several battles, the most decisive of which was at Crécy in 1346. It is recorded that, to transport his army to France, the Hamble River was able to supply 18 vessels crewed by 325 men. By comparison, Portsmouth supplied five ships and 96 men.

In 1354 a Charter, a written privilege granted by the Sovereign, Edward III, was given to Roger de Mortimer, Earl of March, and his heirs. This entitled him to hold a weekly market on Mondays 'at his town of Hamelhoke' and a yearly fair there on the nativity of St. John the Baptist (midsummer day). The Earl's men were also entitled to 'put into port of that town with their ships and other vessels laden with any merchandise not belonging to the staple* and to discharge and sell the merchandise or otherwise dispose of it, paying dues to the collectors of customs at Southampton'.

It was at a house in Hamble in 1415 that the Earl of Cambridge, Sir Thomas Grey and Lord Scrope of Masham met to work out the final details of their conspiracy to get rid of Henry V and place the Earl of March† upon the throne. Henry was at Southampton, preparatory to sailing for France and Agincourt, and ships to carry the army across the Channel were assembled ready at Southampton, Hamble and Portchester. It is recorded that Henry visited the ships at Portchester but does not appear to have come to Hamble. There was much coming and going for several days as the conspirators and the Earl of March met in Hamble and discussed their plans.

The plot, however, was discovered. Sir Thomas Grey wrote his confession and he, Cambridge and Scrope were beheaded at the Bargate in Southampton.

At this time the Hamble River had a boom defence. This consisted of a small wooden fort by the Oyster Hard with a chain stretching across the River. Part of the chain was found in the mud in 1922.

Throughout the years, the name of Hamble appears again and again, sometimes in connection with royalty or the nobility and their visits, for one reason or another, at other times casual mentions of some mundane matter. It is well to bear in mind that Winchester was the capital of Wessex from the 9th century and William I made it his capital in 1066. The Domesday Book was compiled there as the returns came in from the shires. Its decline as a capital began about 1150 and, by 1338, it had lost its status.

Hamble is but 12 miles from Winchester and so there need be no great surprise at the numerous references made to the village. By studying snatches of detailed information, it is possible to build in one's mind a picture of what life was like for those who lived in the village.

As examples, we get a busy picture when we learn from Pipe Rolls that in 1413 the '*Saint Mark* of Brittany was captured by a King's subject contrary to the truce between the King's father and Brittany and taken to Hamell in the possession of Thomas Bromwych'. The 'Serjeant of Arms' was sent to persuade him to return the ship – or to be arrested.

In 1414 ships and mariners at Hamble were commandeered to convey the King's ambassadors and their servants to Brittany. By 1417 many vessels were laid up at Hamble and instructions were given 'to take 6 mariners for the governance and safe keeping of said ship now in port of Hamele'. The vessels listed were the ships *Jesus*, *Holigost* and *La Trinity*, the carracks *Petre*, *Poule*, *Andrew*, *Christofre*, *Marie of Hamele*, *George*, *Marie of Sandewyche* each to have 6 caretakers and the ships *Marie* and *Christofre* 3 each.

From Henry VII's 'accounts and inventry' we learn that the *Grace Dieu* (the second) was brought into dock of Hamill on the Hoke on 10th October 1485. On the same date, the *Governor* was in the River and, on 11th October, *Marie de la Tour* came, preparatory to a voyage to the Mediterranean the following year. We learn, too, that in building Portsmouth dry dock a payment was made to 'John Clarke of Tychfeld, Maister of Harvy Hawards Ship of Hamyll coming out of Spayne on 22nd July 1485 for 2 tonne of chosyn yron price per tonne £4'.

'A hundred of board from Hammel to Portsmouth for the repair of the Sovereign 1496-7.'

'Thomas Harris of Hamel supplied a small cablet of 2 cwt. price 9/- per cwt. and Thomas Harris the elder DC weight ropes.'

In 1497 Harvy Haward 'maister of the *Regent*' was paid 3/4 by the week, John Eustus and Thomas Hoker‡ fifteen pence per week and other mariners 1/- per week. In the same year we read that 'at the edyfying and Newmaking of Our Sovereign Lord the Kings Newbarke *Sweppstake* Thomas Jourde of Crofton supplied the wood for the keel and stems,' other wood coming from Hambledon, Fareham, Tychfeld, Botley, etc., while Thomas Harries of Hammel supplied 2 cwt. of 'okome', Harvy Haward her mainmast and Harris a 'parell with 16 polleys for Takles.' A parrel was the rope by which the centres of yards were fastened to the mast so as to allow the yard to slide up and down.

The old ropemaker's cottage, in which a Harries still lived in the early 1900s, stood at the entrance to Taylor's Wharf until the late 1970s, when it was demolished.

In 1528 the *Gabriel Royal* was docked in the River and in 1545 part of the fleet was ordered to be laid up at Hamble.

In 1576 a Southampton boatman was hired to take a number of men to their ship at Hamble. On the way, they seized a ship and drove the crew overboard with daggers and swords. The boatman escaped when the pirates went ashore at Arundel. In

---

*Staple: a town or place appointed by royal authority in which was a body of merchants having the exclusive right of purchase of certain classes of goods destined for export.

† The Earl of March was descended from the second son of Edward III and therefore had the prior claim to the English throne over Henry V, descended from Edward's third son.

‡ Members of the Hooker family have lived in Hamble ever since and in January 1937 Mrs. Sarah Hooker celebrated her 92nd birthday by serving behind the bar of the Whyte Harte, claiming to be the oldest licensee in Britain.

Rope Walk (formerly Back Street), showing the chapel, 1890. Ropemaker's cottage is on the right.

1606 there was another case of piracy. A number of men were put aboard the *Grace of God* in the Itchen one night. She was then towed to Hamble. When giving evidence to the Southampton Justices, the boatman denied taking any part in seizing the vessel.

In 1577 there was a complaint against John Fry, a farmer of Hamble, that he had 'a cove and byes oysters of them that comes from the sea and kepes them in his cove and selleth them againe having no crafte at sea at all . . .'. The fishermen apparently resented a farmer having a hand in their business.

Admiralty Court records mention one Owen Symons of Hamble as being a 'usual conveyor of wood beyond the seas' in 1579 and at that time 'at Hamble divers barkes is laden with wood to be transported to the great hinderans and great dearth of the same'.

Sir Henry Mainwaring, who in his younger days was a pirate, was a seaman through and through (he was also a B.A. Cantab., M.D. Oxon, and a student of the Inner Temple). He obtained a pardon for his lapse into piracy and was made Governor of St. Andrew's Castle on Hamble Common. His knowledge of seafaring matters was unsurpassed and in 1612 his advice was sought by the Admiralty concerning the location of a Naval base. He chose Portsmouth and gave as one of his reasons that it was near Hamble, no doubt because of the River's comfortable anchorage, its comparative safety from raids and the existence of personnel to repair and maintain ships laid up there. He later became an Admiral and Deputy Lord Warden of the Cinq Ports.

Hamble Lands

In man's early days of civilization and settlement, he inherited old tribal customs. He lived in a free community where individual ownership of land did not exist. The family or group used what the land provided and organized themselves to make the most of it.

By custom, each man's duties and rights became established and deeply rooted. They were necessary for good management so every man was given his job and told in what way he had to help others in collective work.

Over this system lay the power of a conqueror whose rule was law and who, to reward those who had helped him militarily or had rendered some other service, would grant them limited powers over certain parts of his domain. Such people might, in their turn, make similar lesser awards to those who had pleased them or perhaps to those whose loyalty they wished to ensure.

The Lord of the Manor might be the King or a bishop or someone to whom the manor had been granted. He held the manor 'in trust' rather than owned it in a modern sense and both he and the peasants had to comply with ancient custom so far as the working of the estate was concerned, for these customs were necessary for good husbandry and were too deeply rooted to disturb.

The manor of Old Hamble was a monastic one, the Bishop of Winchester having granted land to Hamble Priory, but that of Satchell, which is now within the parish boundary, was the manor of Sir Henry Shatershall, a knight of Henry III's day.

The manor consisted of a cluster of houses, a church (St. Andrew's in Hamble and St. Mary's, Hound, for Satchell) and a hall and outbuildings if there was a resident Lord. The estate was divided into three parts: first a Common Field for the cultivation of wheat, oats, beans, turnips or similar crops; second, Common Meadow, which was reserved for hay for winter feed; and third, Common Pasture for grazing cattle, sheep, pigs or horses.

The Common Field was divided into three sections in one of which was grown wheat, another oats, barley or some other crop and the third was left fallow. Each year the crops were rotated.

The sections were further sub-divided into strips, usually marked by a thin strip of unploughed grass, and the farmers or villeins would be granted by the Lord certain strips, some in one field, some in another, and often amounting to several acres altogether. The Lord also 'held' strips and these were cultivated by various villeins or others in the community in return for the lands they held. By custom, each man had rights as well as duties and he guarded them zealously. A man who had cattle or sheep had rights of pasture on the Common waste of the Manor although this was sometimes limited to the number he could graze on his own holding if he were not growing crops at the time.

Next in importance were rights of estovers. This was the right to take certain wood or furze for fuel, very necessary in a cold, damp winter, or turbury rights to cut turf or peat, or to take wood of certain sizes to repair their houses or carts or to dig clay for bricks. Others had the right to collect seaweed from the shore to fertilize their fields. Such a right existed, not only on Hamble and Westfield Commons but also on Tithe 150 which lies along the shore between them. When Shell-Mex pier was built, head-room to drive a cart beneath had to be left for this purpose: hence the strange kink in the pier.

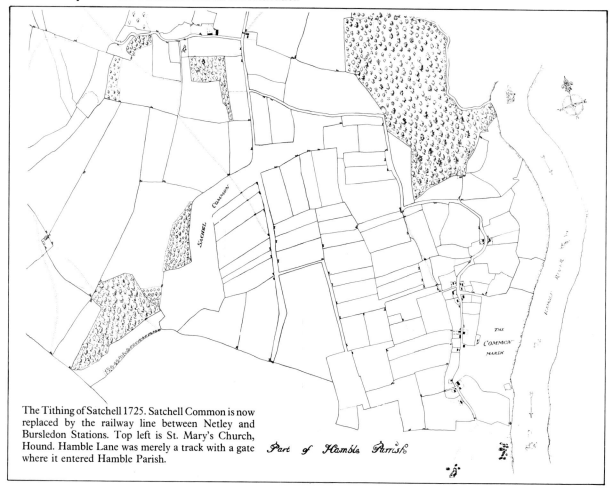

The Tithing of Satchell 1725. Satchell Common is now replaced by the railway line between Netley and Bursledon Stations. Top left is St. Mary's Church, Hound. Hamble Lane was merely a track with a gate where it entered Hamble Parish.

15

Normally there were rights granted to certain people to fish in lakes or rivers but this did not apply in the tidal waters of the parish. The Priory at Hamble did not have any fishponds as at Netley Abbey where the ponds contained vast quantities of fish much needed by the monks and clergy who, up to the 13th century, were forbidden to eat meat at all, eggs, fish and bread being their chief diet.

As well as tending his own strips, the peasant would have to give so many days' work ploughing the Lord's field, so many days' harrowing, reaping, binding, threshing and other tasks necessary to get the best out of the land. Originally this labour was in return for his customary rights but, as time went by, he received meals for his work or could pay a fee instead of performing his duties which, in effect, meant he paid rent for his holding rather than gave his labour.

This system was adhered to for centuries and, even on the map of Satchell of 1725, the fields still show the traditional strips, but by 1838 everything had been changed. The lord of the Manor appointed a steward to run the estate and under him worked a bailiff. The villeins elected one of their number to be reeve, usually the best husbandman, whose job it was to organize the yearly running of the farm. A hayward (hedge warden) was appointed to maintain the hedges and prevent cattle straying from the Common into the cultivated fields. In 1921 the Hamble Parish Council was asked to recommend a hayward for Hamble Common. They were unable to recommend anyone for this position and were subsequently (in 1923) granted control of the Common themselves (this was subsequently revoked and is now controlled by Eastleigh B.C.).

A dey or female servant was in charge of the milking, butter and cheese making, etc., in the deyery (dairy). Examination of the church records shows most of the occupational surnames which one would expect: Taylor, Miller, Baker, Fisher, Cooper, Carter, Wheeler, Brewer, Cook, etc.

As the population grew, more land was taken for agriculture at the expense of the Common grazing area and this was the cause of much resentment by those with cattle. Common Land was nevertheless enclosed.

Then in 1349 came the Black Death which swept the country and drastically reduced the population, with the result that some of the land enclosed for agriculture reverted to waste and it was not for about 150 years that the population again reached the pre-Black Death total. Then the pressure to enclose Common Land was once more exerted and fiercely resisted where it upset the delicate balance of farming.

Until the early 1930s there was a gate across the road at the bottom of School Lane leading on to the Common to prevent cattle from straying.

Life on monastic manors, which were administered by the local Abbot, as in the case of Hamble, was in general more amenable than on a secular one. Good husbandry meant making use of everything of value to the community and very little was wasted. This was accomplished only by good organization, hard work and long hours and the labourers were no doubt relieved to hear the Angelus bell ring out over the fields at dusk as a signal to say a prayer and know that their day's work was done. It was not all work, however, and there were many days in the ecclesiastical calendar when the people could relax.

The feudal system came to an end in the late fifteenth century but the system of husbandry continued. Hamble (or St. Andrew's) Common still retains much of its original boundaries although small pieces have been enclosed from time to time. An attempt was made in the 1920s to enclose Westfield Common but eventually the Commoners' rights were established. The Common Marsh (Oakwood way now stands on what was Common Marsh) off Satchell Lane is now completely enclosed and Satchell Common, which ran from Badnam Copse to Netley Hospital, disappeared before 1838. The pressure now

The Duck Pond and Satchell Marsh with *T.S. Mercury* in the background, about 1900.

being put upon Hamble's Common Lands is not brought about, as in earlier days, by a need for more agricultural land but by the development of housing estates, marinas and industry.

It was as late as 1849 before the ecclesiastical parishes of Hamble and Hound were separated and, although Parish Councils were started in 1772, it was not until the Parish Councils Act of 1894 that Hamble had its own Council. By that Act, a village with a population of more than 300 had to have a Parish Council.

A Parish meeting was duly convened on 4th December 1894 and five councillors were elected by the 27 electors present. Many of the problems which faced the newly elected men (John Scovell (chairman), Charles Brown, Thomas Norris, Albert Penny and Arthur Robinson) are still with us to this day. They included sewerage disposal, the state of footpaths, street lighting (the lamp lighter received £3. 4. 0. per annum for storing and lighting the lamps) and repairs to the hards. There were obstructed rights-of-way to be kept open and many other subjects which never seem to leave us.

By 1901 there were complaints about traffic in Hamble Lane causing danger at Sydney (now Coronation) Corner and in 1921 the Parish Council had to ask the Southampton Harbour Board to make a by-law prohibiting steamers from pumping out their bilges and polluting the water to the detriment of the fishing industry and bathers.

Some of the early worries, however, have passed with the years. Among these may be listed the nuisance caused by fair stalls and whirligigs (roundabouts) on the Quay, the necessity to prohibit the washing of clothes at the village pump in Well Lane because of the pollution caused and the need to clear excessive amounts of seaweed washed up on the foreshore.

The Hamble civil boundaries were extended in 1902 to include Satchell at the request of the residents of that tithing and the ecclesiastical boundaries followed suit in 1910.

The village's struggle to maintain the Commoners' rights and open spaces has been long and hard. Control of Hamble Green was gained in 1901 and in 1923 the Commons Scheme giving the parish control of the Common and Green came into effect. This was exercised until 1955.

Attempts were made in 1924 to enclose Westfield Common and a gate was placed across the top of Coach Road which was then a magnificent avenue of great beeches. The ensuing battle over common and copyhold rights was eventually won and the gate removed.

Over the years, as Parish Councils have proved their worth, they have acquired more powers and responsibilities and have steadily raised the standard of local government.

Hamble's Village Green consists of 2.1 acres (the average size of Greens in England is just under 3 acres) and, like most Greens, it is probably 1,000 to 1,500 years old. They were probably established for the protection of all livestock of the community during temporary emergencies. In times of strife, when cattle were likely to be rustled, they could be driven in from the outlying Commons to the centre of the village for protection. There are fewer than 1,400 Greens left in England and they are unevenly distributed, being most dense in Hertfordshire, but Hampshire is also well endowed.

As times became more settled, the Village Green lost its original purpose and became used for sport, particularly archery, a sport encouraged by Edward III (1363) and others up to Henry VIII in 1509. Gradually they became the peaceful Greens we know today, being used for children's games and the occasional fair or even for just sitting and contemplating their antiquity.

Hamble was one of the smallest parishes and not a great agricultural area. Few worked the land, as may be judged from the acreage returns for 1801 which give Wheat 40, Barley 40, Oats 5, Potatoes ½, Peas 8, Beans nil, Turnips 20 and Rye nil.

View from the Manor House across the Village Green and Common. The Ha-Ha can just be seen.

Villagers on the Quay, Regatta Day about 1870, some of them are sitting on crab boxes.

The Duck Pond by Satchell Farm, about 1900.

Satchell Farm and outbuildings 1925.

This general pattern continued for the next 100 years or so. Farmer Brown was a great sheep farmer and, until 1909, some 300 sheep were kept on Manor Farm. His shepherd, Joels, lived in a tiny cottage (now greatly enlarged and named "Folly's End") opposite the Mercury while Sharp, the carter, whose job it was to look after the horses and cope with the ploughing, lived at thatched Yew Tree Cottage in Satchell Lane (Fulwood is now on the site of Yew Tree Cottage), with a sheep-dip just over the road. Shearing was always done at Manor Farm.

Satchell Farm maintained a herd of 20-30 cows and Manor Farm usually had 30-40, although in about 1920 this had increased to about 80, but by then there was no sheep. Mr. Bartlett then ran the farm and, apart from his large family, who all worked, he employed two cowmen, two carters and a boy and two labourers.

The new part of Manor Farm was built about 200 years ago but the old farm, now the kitchen, is very much older.

Yew Tree Cottage, Satchell Lane, replaced by Fulwood, about 1920.

The Geography of Hamble

Old maps of the area have provided much useful information about Hamble. In the Municipal Library of Pirano, Istria, there is a wood engraving by Pietri Coppo dating from about 1500. It shows the British Isles – Scotland as a separate island – and a dozen or so towns. These include Hamble (Ambua) and Southampton (Antina). The map appears to have been for the use of Italian seamen trading with England as the few towns mentioned are coastal. Winchester, for instance, is not shown. The map is very inaccurate but the very inclusion of Hamble is a clue to its importance so far as sailors were concerned. A safe anchorage in sheltered waters at the end of a long voyage will always be an attraction.

Saxton's Map of Hampshire in 1575 shows Hamble Haven looking rather larger than it is today, with the mouth of the river slightly to the westward. The villages of Hamble, Hoke and Hound are shown as is St. Andrew's (St. Andros) Castle on Hamble Common. 'Brusilerfery' appears up river but no indication of a ferry at Hamble. Warsash and Swanwick do not appear although Kirbridge and Botley do.

Johan Blaeu's map of Hantonia (or Hantshire) dated 1648 also shows St. Andrew's Castle and Hamble Haven. The neighbouring villages of Berseldon, Swenwyk and Warmanshe, Hooke and Shatsham also appear.

John Speede's map of Hantshire (1607) shows Hamble River, Hooke, Hamble, St. Andrews Castle, Shatshel, Warmanshe, Berseldon, Swenewijk, Kirbridg and Boteley. It also shows that Hamble was in Mansbridge Hundred. 'Hundreds' were introduced into England by King Alfred (871 – 901) and were Danish in origin. It was a division of a county and was so called because the division could be obliged to find 100 able-bodied men to keep the King's peace within the area or for war purposes. It was sub-divided into Manors.

A 1725 estate map of Hound shows details of all fields and owners or tenants in that parish. At that time, Hamble's northern boundary ran from the northern edge of the grounds of Riverside (now the R.A.F. Yacht Club), across the fields by the College of Air Training's sports field to Lovers' Lane and Netley Hospital grounds. Hamble Lane, from the junction with Satchell Lane to Lovers' Lane was then an unmetalled track with a gate and stile across it.

The main road to Hamble appears to have been by way of Satchell Lane. Satchell was the estate of Sir Henry Shatershall, a knight of Henry III (1216 – 1272) and was a separate tithing but came under the parish of Hound until the boundary change in 1902. The tithing was released by Henry III from all service at the shire and hundred courts and from payment of all scot[1] and geld[2] and tolls. The only buildings in the tithing in 1725 were Satchell Farm and a few cottages. In 1795 the population was 27. To the river side of the Lane lay Common Marsh which extended to the river bank but this was enclosed before 1838.

Satchell Common was a long, narrow area running from Badnam Copse to Netley Hospital but this, too, does not appear as 'Common' in the 1797 map or the 1838 Tithe Map of Hound. The main cultivated area, that now occupied by the aerodrome, was divided into numerous 'strip' fields, probably, as was usual under feudal agricultural practice, with turf banks in place of hedges. By 1797 these small fields had given way to much larger ones.

A 1797 survey map shows the public footpath to the west of Satchell Lane as it was in 1725 and also shows the one across the

[1]payment, especially for hospitality, hence 'scot free'.
[2](land tax paid to the Crown).

Hampton Cottages, Hamble Lane, about 1910.

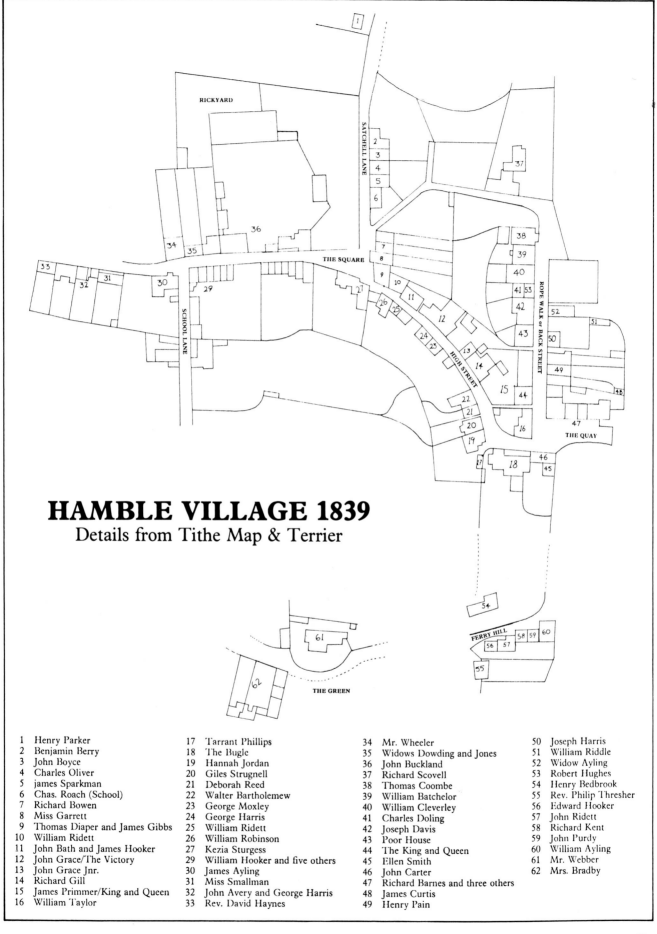

HAMBLE VILLAGE 1839
Details from Tithe Map & Terrier

1　Henry Parker
2　Benjamin Berry
3　John Boyce
4　Charles Oliver
5　james Sparkman
6　Chas. Roach (School)
7　Richard Bowen
8　Miss Garrett
9　Thomas Diaper and James Gibbs
10　William Ridett
11　John Bath and James Hooker
12　John Grace/The Victory
13　John Grace Jnr.
14　Richard Gill
15　James Primmer/King and Queen
16　William Taylor

17　Tarrant Phillips
18　The Bugle
19　Hannah Jordan
20　Giles Strugnell
21　Deborah Reed
22　Walter Bartholemew
23　George Moxley
24　George Harris
25　William Ridett
26　William Robinson
27　Kezia Sturgess
29　William Hooker and five others
30　James Ayling
31　Miss Smallman
32　John Avery and George Harris
33　Rev. David Haynes

34　Mr. Wheeler
35　Widows Dowding and Jones
36　John Buckland
37　Richard Scovell
38　Thomas Coombe
39　William Batchelor
40　William Cleverley
41　Charles Doling
42　Joseph Davis
43　Poor House
44　The King and Queen
45　Ellen Smith
46　John Carter
47　Richard Barnes and three others
48　James Curtis
49　Henry Pain

50　Joseph Harris
51　William Riddle
52　Widow Ayling
53　Robert Hughes
54　Henry Bedbrook
55　Rev. Philip Thresher
56　Edward Hooker
57　John Ridett
58　Richard Kent
59　John Purdy
60　William Ayling
61　Mr. Webber
62　Mrs. Bradby

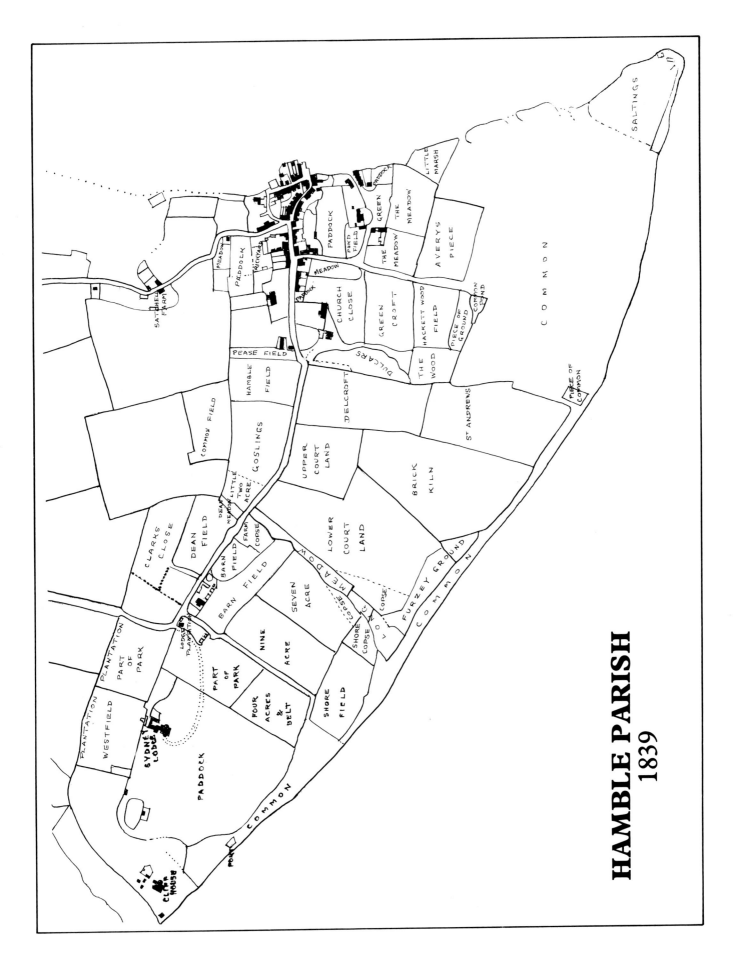

HAMBLE PARISH
1839

22

aerodrome which was abolished during the Second World War. This latter footpath connected Hamble and Hound churches but that part across the aerodrome is not shown in 1725.

In Hamble, as is usual in country districts, most public footpaths led to the Church. This was not entirely due to the piety of the inhabitants but to an old custom that where a body was carried became a right-of-way and those carrying a coffin naturally took the shortest route across the fields to the church.

However, in 1935 the Courts held that there was no basis in law to support such a claim. The belief that there was such a right, however, was widespread and there can be little doubt that many paths owe their existence to the mistake.

The names of the various fields can be found in the schedules which accompany the tithe maps and some have been preserved in the names of housing estates and houses such as Deanfield Close, Westfield, Dulcars (the former Vicarage), and Barnfield. The schedules tell, too, what was grown in each field that year and which were pasture.

The Norman Tower, St. Andrew's.

The Old Rectory, 1821.

The Parish Church

The Benedictine Priory of St. Andrew was a cell or branch of the great Abbey of Tyrone or Thiron, near Chartres. It is generally accepted that it was established by St. Bernard of Thiron who, on his visit to England, probably founded the priory at Hamble himself in about 1100 A.D. He died in 1116. It is possible, however, that part of the building is of earlier Saxon origin and recent excavations have verified this.

The church was consecrated in 1109 by William Gifford, Bishop of Winchester (1098-1128), who gave the Monks of St. Andrew a hide of land, that is as much as could be tilled in a year by a single plough or as much land as could be enclosed by a thong cut from one hide, probably about 80-100 acres.

The community was never a large one, probably only about six monks. By a charter of Henry II (1154-1189), the Monks of Hamble were exempt from toll, passage, pontage (a toll paid for the use of a bridge), etc., in England and Normandy. They were also granted various pensions by high personages and the Monks of St. Swithun's at Winchester supplied them with habits, shoes, boots, loaves and ale. In return, each mid-Lent, the Hamble Monks sent 20,000 oysters to their Winchester brethren. There were occasional disputes when the Hamble Monks did not get their provisions.

The priory, whose mother house was in France, was, of course, regarded as alien and, during the French wars in 1294, the lands were seized by Edward I. At that time the Prior held a house, garden and dovecote valued at 4/- a year, 79 acres of land, 13/8, 8 acres of meadow, 5/4, pannage (feeding ground for swine in woodland) over 4 acres, 18d, and wood necessary for house repairs and fences. There were also four free-tenants holding 21 acres, paying an annual rental of 6/-, 27 customary tenants

Early engraving of St. Andrew's.

In 1352 Edward III granted an annuity of 10 marks to Agnes Pore, a nurse to his daughter Margaret, to be paid yearly from the farm of the Priory of Hamble so long as the war with France continued. Richard II reaffirmed this payment when he came to the throne.

In 1360 John de Roier, Abbot of St. Mary de Artisis, was appointed Proctor in England of the possessions of the Abbey of Thiron. There still exists a lease, dated 13 Edward II (1320), which bears the seal of the Prior of Hamble. It is in dark green wax, pointed oval, 1⅜ inches long, depicting the martyrdom of St. Andrew, with a moon and star on each side and a praying monk in the base, and bears the legend 'S. Priors de Hamele'.

In 1371, Bishop William of Wykeham granted the custody of the Priory to William de Salarium, a monk of Thiron. William de Foxele was Prior from 1375-1390. In 1377 the French raided the South Coast and the Priory of Hamble suffered from their plundering. When there was a similar threat some years later (1404), Winchester College provided soldiers but this precaution proved unnecessary.

In 1390 there was a vacancy and the Abbot of Thiron presented two clerks to the Bishop who instituted one of them, John Beel, to the Priory. The known Priors of Hamble were: Geoffrey 1135, Alan 1313, Richard de Floris –, John de Estrepaniacho 1318-22, Richard de Beaumont 1322-45, James Pasquier 1345, William de Monsteriis –, William de Foxele 1375-90, John Beel 1391.

Edward III (1327-77) had shorn the alien priories of much of their glory and Henry V (1413-22) finally suppressed them. They had become of little value to their mother houses which were probably glad to get rid of them when there was an offer to purchase. In this way, William of Wykeham came by much of the property with which he endowed the two St. Mary Colleges (Oxford and Winchester).

holding four acres and paying 28/4 but whose labour was worth nothing, and 16 cottars (occupier of a cottage belonging to a farm) who paid 12d per year. The total annual value of the priory was reckoned at £18.14.8.

Winchester College hold a copy of a bull of Pope Innocent II confirming the Abbots of Thiron in possession of the churches which had been given to the Abbey. These include 'St. Andrew de Anglia'.

One of the grounds for complaint about alien priories was that they paid a sort of tribute to the parent monastery which meant sending money abroad.

St. Andrew's about 1900.

Interior of St. Andrew's. The East Window was a casualty in the Second World War.

Hamble was vested in the St. Mary College, Winchester in 1391 and remains so today.

The Church of the Priory is now the parish church and there are but few traces of the Priory. Much of the church is Norman although it was largely rebuilt by Winchester College early in the fifteenth century.

The north doorway is a fine example of the transition between Norman and Early English architecture with fine zig-zag moulding. The tower is Norman. The door (now on the out-side of the porch, having been moved from the inside by a vicar in the 1960s) is thought to be the original one and contains many knife cuts. The men of Hamble were largely seamen and it was their custom, when about to undertake a hazardous voyage, to pray at the church for a safe return. They then made a vertical knife cut on the wooden door. On returning, if they did return, they gave thanks for their safe delivery and turned their original mark into a cross by making a short horizontal cut. Robert Williams, who died in 1932, and George Penny are two who made such cuts. Those in the Royal Navy cut a triangle and a small circle about one of the angles, depending upon whether they were to serve in the home, West Indian or Mediterranean fleets.

In 1760 a west gallery was erected to accommodate the large congregation who drew lots for seats. The gallery was taken down in 1879.

There are three bells in the tower: the two smaller were cast in 1715. The largest is inscribed 'A.O.U.G.A.P.T.; the other 'Amos Bradby, Churchwarden, Clement Tosier cast me in the year 1715'; the smallest: 'Lettel and small tho I ham, but I will be heard above all. CT 1715'. The Angelus bell also bears the inscription 'AU GRACIAP' which is a shortened version of 'Ave Maria Gracia plena'.

The clock itself was given by Martha Janverin in 1878 in memory of her husband. There are a number of memorials in the church to members of the Janverin family.

Among the many interesting gravestones in the church-yard are some with ship illustrations. That of Sir Alliott Verdon Roe proclaims him as 'the first Englishman to fly'. Sir Alliott was a brother of a former Vicar of Hamble. There is also a gravestone inscribed in Chinese. This is the last resting place of a Chinese student pilot at Air Service Training, Ltd., who died of Asian 'flu shortly after the last war.

The earliest register dates from 1660 and this contains entries not only for Hamble but for Hound, Satchell, Netley and

Common Pond with the old Rectory and St. Andrew's Church in the background.

Sholing as well. This appears to be because the vicars of the parish of Hound, which included Hamble, Bursledon and Sholing, lived at Hamble for several centuries and ran the whole parish from there, with the help of curates. Hamble did not become a separate ecclesiastical parish until 1862.

By studying these records of births, baptisms, marriages and deaths it is possible to trace through the centuries old Hamble family names, such as Taylor, Hooker, Ayling, Sparshott, Bedbrook, Cousins (spelt in various ways), Cooper, Baker, Bradby, Barfoot. Many strangers were buried, probably seamen from other places – Henry Adams was a common name given to seamen whose names were unknown. The field known as Avery's Piece dates back to one of that name buried in 1682. Other names, such as Janverin and Scovell, men of importance in their day, have died out in the village while Williams and Bevis do not appear in the older records. There were several deaths during the Plague so it appears that the village did not escape.

During the French wars in 1795, two French soldiers married girls in the village.

There is also mention of a Court Leet (a court of record held periodically in a hundred, lordship or manor, before the lord or his steward and attended by the residents of the district) and Baron (assembly of the freehold tenants of a manor under the presidency of the lord or his steward) held in Hamblerice in 1810. The Gun House was known as Murford's and had a brewhouse attached. A John Murford married in 1667 and the name is mentioned again in 1701. From these old records we also learn that William Ayling was a 'marriner' and chemist, James Ayling a fishing smack owner, George St. Barbe another 'marriner' and Charles Scovell a sailmaker. In 1735 John Johnston was the Salt Officer – the Salt House was on land now occupied by Hamble Point Marina and Cougar Marine.

Headstones in Hamble Churchyard

River Life

The Oyster Hard was so called because a large mound of oyster shells existed close to the south of it. This great heap was surrounded by mud and had a small clump of rushes growing on top. At first it would appear that generations of fishermen had tossed the dead or poor specimens overboard and the shells had accumulated. This is possible but it would have been difficult to get a laden keeled boat so close inshore owing to her draught, except at very high spring tides, and no self-respecting skipper would risk being beneaped.

Other such mounds existed. One recently disappeared with the building of Port Hamble's marina, another was by the public right-of-way in front of the R.A.F. Yacht Club. One is left wondering whether they are the sites of the habitation of early water people who built their homes on stilts over the water. Similar mounds in Sweden are thought to be such remains.

Oysters must have been plentiful in the area for hundreds of years. Each mid-Lent from 1292 the monks at St. Andrew's sent 20,000 of them to their brethren at Winchester. Local oyster beds were productive until about 1870. Large fleets of oyster boats, sometimes 20-30 strong, from Colchester and the East Coast would visit Hamble for the season until the Hamble beds were over-dredged and no oysters were left. The industry failed

and it was nearly 100 years before oysters returned in marketable quantities.

Fishing and Hamble have travelled side by side at least since the 15th century and her sons have gone down to the sea in ships and seen the wonders of the Lord. A Portsmouth newspaper of 1765 records that 'on Monday there was brought into Hamble, in a lobster smack, a fish of monstrous size, said to be a grampus, that weighed five tons and produced eight hogsheads of oil'.

When the oyster business died, the attention of local fishermen turned to spratting in the winter and yachts in summer. The sprats were packed in hampers at Quay House (now part of the Royal Southern Yacht Club) and taken by wagon and four horses to market. In 1893 there were 22 spratters on the River with a total crew of 80 men. Before long, however, sprats went out of dietetic fashion and the men were sometimes unable to sell their catches which were then used as manure on Warsash fields. By 1924 there were only two or three spratters left.

Scallop dredging followed, mostly in Caen Bay during winter months. Tales of the hardship of wresting a living from the sea are general and scallop dredging seems to have been one of the toughest ways of making a living. The best weather for

Fisherman George Penney at Hamble. 'Sometimes I just sits and thinks, sometimes I just sits.'

The Quay and Lukes' yard in 1905 with two crabbers.

good catches was when it was bitterly cold with ice quickly forming on the spray-covered smack, for a good wind was needed to blow her sideways, this being how the heavy dredges were towed. In these conditions, the men had to handle nets made of iron rings which bit into the seabed as she crabbed her way to leeward. Then back to Hamble, a quick turn-round and a hard slog across the Channel to the fishing grounds again.

Crabbing also had its moments and there was a steady trade with the West Country and Ireland from about 1870 to 1920. Vessels had to be converted for this work. The hold amidships was sealed off with watertight bulkheads and holes drilled in the bottom and sides to flood her and provide storage for live crabs which were collected from various places to the west. They were not caught by the crew but by the local fishermen.

In due course this trade, too, came to an end and the crabbers were put into mud berths and there most of them ended their days for it was well-nigh impossible to float them again as mud squeezed through the holes and filled the holds, sinking them still deeper into the mud. There they remain, some no more than a few ribs and stem and stern post, a memorial to fine seamen, tough and hardworking, who saw their families through difficult times or died in the attempt.

Casualties were heavy for profits were small and it was necessary to keep working, even in bad weather. On a return trip from Southern Ireland, one crabber carried away her rudder off Start Point in a gale but sailed on to the Hamble, steering by putting the longboat over the side and towing it broadside with two warps which were constantly manned. The *Imogene*, a Hamble schooner, was lost with all hands in 1903 in a North Sea gale. The *Laurel* was another Hamble vessel which sank in the

North Sea but her crew were lucky to be picked up by a steamer. Many were drowned at sea and several smacks sank. As time caught up with the old vessels, they were laid up on the mud and left to rot.

One such was the *Ceres* and her career was similar to that of many other craft based at Hamble. She was built at Poole in 1869, registered SU2, 49 tons (MNL 62411). She was one of a fleet of four built for the grain trade with the Channel Islands. On her maiden voyage, she grounded on Kimmeridge Ledge and was badly holed. A crew from Hamble salvaged her with the aid of empty oil drums and she was fitted with a crab well.

The crab well on *Ceres* was 20 feet long and amidships, taking up her full beam of 18 feet, and the depth in hold 6 feet. Holes were drilled, about 1½ inches in diameter, between the ribs at frequent intervals. There were, of course, watertight bulkheads at the fore and after ends of the well. Just above the waterline and on either side of the well there was a well deck giving about 4 feet headroom under the main deck. Here trawls and other fishing gear were stowed. Crabs were loaded through the well and taken alive to the Hamble where they were kept in ponds or afloat in great boxes called caves (pronounced carves), a name borrowed from the French, meaning cellars.

Ceres spent the rest of her life as a crabber, although she saw brief service on other business. She dredged scallops in Caen Bay. On one typical trip she left Hamble on Friday and returned on Monday with 24,000 scallops (100 bags of 20 dozen) which she had brought up from the bottom of Caen Bay.

The crabs came mainly from Southern Ireland but the French coast and the West Country were fairly widely used. *Ceres* also brought lobsters and crayfish from Ireland and Norway and oysters from Whitstable after the local beds were

HAMBLE FROM THE AIR.

Aerial view of the lower village and riverside.

The crabber Ceres, built 1869.

fished out. She normally worked five drudges (a dredger for dredging up shellfish) which were lashed with plaited ropes and toggles to stanchions.

Charles Saunders of Southampton was her owner in 1869 and her skipper was red-bearded Robert Williams, known throughout the village as 'Uncle Bob'. (He was, in fact, related to very many of the villagers. 'Uncle Bob's Cup', presented by him to Hamble River Sailing Club in 1927, with the object of encouraging the younger generation to sail, has been raced for ever since, except during the war years.) He retired before the First World War after 35 years as her captain. With a Hamble crew under him, he had kept her as spick and span as any yacht. She had a winch on either side of the mast for drudges and halliards, her peak halliard was chain. Her main and mizzen were rather square-headed and she carried a jib-headed topsail.

She appears in the Mercantile Navy List of 1924 as 'fitted with auxiliary motors'. From 1925-29 she was owned by B.C.A. Scott but was not listed in 1930.

In common with others in the trade, Ceres could not always come straight into the river on arrival, for crayfish and lobsters do not like fresh water and, after heavy rain, the water in the river and crab ponds was not to their liking. This meant that the crabbers often had to lay off by the Spit Buoy for a while, which was not at all welcome for she would normally expect to make twenty round trips in a summer.

Her dimensions were: length 66 ft; depth in hold 6 ft; beam 19 ft; 39 tons net, 52 gross. What remains of her lies in the mud north of Port Hamble's marina.

The Jubilee was another vessel converted for the crab trade. She was a schooner of 31 tons built at Ayr in 1857 and had been a yacht until 1887. In 1910 she was managed and owned by Charles Saunders and continued to work until 1923. In 1924 she was laid up on the mud off Hamble Common. Her fastest trip was of 4½ days from Hamble to Waterford, load and return.

The Peri was also a schooner. She had been built in Prince Edward Island in 1848 but underwent extensive refit and was lengthened and raised at Salcombe. A three-masted schooner, she was the longest in the crab trade. Her owners were Scovells of Hamble Fisheries for whom she brought some of the first crabs from Concarneau but this trade declined about 1888. She had carried 'fish' from Norway and had been aground on the Goodwins but got off again. The term 'fish' included shellfish, crabs, lobsters, etc.

The Peri finished up on the mud in Luke's yard where the staging leading to the old pontoon was built over her. The remains were cleared away by Port Hamble in 1947.

The Ellen had a reputation for being a fast yawl. She was built in Southampton in 1840, a 36-tonner owned by the Scovells. Like the Peri, she was lengthened at Hamble in 1867-68. She returned from the Fastnet, covering the 400 miles in 49 hours, though this was not claimed as a record, others having done the trip in 40 hours. She was laid to rest alongside the Ceres.

The Cupid was a 28-ton ketch built at Bembridge in 1822 as an I.O.W. pilot boat but was bought by Charles Saunders and fitted with a fish well at Warsash. She last appeared in the M.N. List in 1922, after which she was laid up on the mud next to the Jubilee. Her skipper was Mark Spink of Warsash.

Secret was a 21-ton smack built in 1864 and owned by Robert Scovell Jnr. of Hamble. She had been a spratter but was derelict on Hamble Common mud from 1890. Ariel, like the Cupid, was an old Bembridge Pilot boat. She had been built clinker (the lower edge of every plank overlaps that next below it) but was replanked carvel (planks are all flush and smooth, the edges laid close to each other and caulked to make them watertight) by Moodys in about 1873 and was still fishing in 1923.

The Jane was a smack built at the Hamble Boatyard at Fairey's point when it was Scovell's and had dredged oysters in the North Sea. She was copper-fastened and, when put ashore off Fairey's, soon broke up because people took the copper bolts out of her. Fairey's concrete slipway is built over her remains which lie so few yards from her birthplace.

The Margaret, Result and Active were another three smacks of the Scovell fleet. Cargo and McFisher were a couple of ketches, still crabbing in 1924, while Zebedee, which had brought crabs and lobsters from France and Ireland, took station alongside the Jane and had completely disappeared by 1923.

The Albion, a one-time spratter, had carried cider from Totnes and potatoes from France and eventually took her place on the mud at Warsash, alongside the old crabber Eagle and the Stella. Nearby was the Gipsy Queen whose skipper was Captain Foy. His daughter was born aboard her and later married Austin Hooker who became landlord of the Bugle Inn.

Mary Leak was another crabber which finished on the mud off Port Hamble, while the ketch Gem in 1924 was still bringing crabs and crayfish to Warsash. She then had an auxiliary engine. Later she was used by Luke's yachtyard for lifting masts out of yachts, thence to the mud near the Ceres, but she was subsequently taken to the Itchen where she sank just downstream of Northam Bridge.

The smacks Emma and Star were both broken up shortly after the first World War. Imogene and Laurel were both lost at sea.

The Racer was another spratter still working in 1924. She had been built in Guernsey in 1859 and finished on the mud above Bursledon Bridge near the New Hope which had been sailed to France by Moody in 1870 with a cargo of pig iron from smelting works below Warsash. New Hope was built in about 1833 by a Capt. Croucher of Cowes for trade between Southampton, Portsmouth and the Isle of Wight. She was lengthened at Cowes and had carried flowers from the Scillies, granite from Cornwall and flour from Botley.

There are two other wrecks on the mud of the Hamble River, just above the old Mercury pier. They are not local trading vessels but two North Sea trawlers, one the Flash, built at Great Yarmouth, the other the Fortuna, built at Hull. Both were put ashore by the Training School and used as fever and hospital ships.

There had been a flourishing trade in which some 12 or 13 ships of various rigs – brigs, brigantines and schooners – had taken grain to and flour from Botley Mill which it is claimed has existed for over 1,000 years and was mentioned in Domesday Book. They would go as far as Bursledon Pool where their cargo was loaded into lighters and poled up to the mill. The lighters were taken through a tunnel under the road at a critical state of the tide. If it was too low, there was not sufficient water to float and, if too high, not sufficient headroom to pass under. At night a boy would lower a lamp at the far end so that the boatman could judge his time and be able to see what he was about. Flour was taken away by the same method at tenpence a sack.

The schooner *Comet* (Capt. Jewel) was lost with all hands off Fowey on passage from Botley to Penzance. This waterborne trade eased somewhat with the coming of the railway to Botley in 1842 but did not finally die until the First World War. From 1860 to 1900 flour was shipped to the Isle of Wight, Portsmouth and Southampton.

Most of the output of gravel and moulders' loam from Badnam was taken away by sea in brigantines and schooners until the early 1920s. These vessels brought coal, mainly from Sunderland, to Southampton and were towed to Hamble to load loam to act as ballast for the return voyage. The loam was in demand in the north-east for moulds for iron castings. Pit-props were also taken on the return journey.

Coal was brought to the River by two schooners of about 300 tons, the *Waterwitch* and *McBain*, which sailed from the north-east coast, lay to buoys at Bursledon and unloaded into lighters, while two spritsail barges, the *Cambria* and *Brittanic*, also from the east coast, put themselves ashore at Warsash to unload. From 1892 the barge *Spec*, with 20 tons trans-shipped at Southampton, brought coal to Moody's on spring tide only, and to Taylor's Wharf at Hamble. The *Spec* was followed by the spritty *Mary Emily* (J. Williams) and later by the 40-ton ketch *Exchange*.

Shipbuilding

There can be no doubt that shipbuilding on the Hamble River has been going on since time immemorial. Details of the King's ships are well documented but not those of small trading or fishing boats. Those who carve a precarious living out of the sea need ships. These were limited in size for the builders did not trust joins in keels and consequently early vessels were restricted by the size of the tree.

Henry V's *Grace Dieu* was experimental in this respect and was distrusted by many seamen of her day. It was over 200 years before such a large ship was again built. Her remains lie in the

Shipbuilding 1920 style on the Hamble. The busy building yard of Luke Bros. near to the Quay.

mud upriver and were long thought to be those of a Viking ship but this theory was exploded in 1934 when experts examined 'The Bursledon Ship' and the Government records. She proved to be the *Grace Dieu of the Tower* (the Tower being the Tower of London; 'of the Tower' signified much the same as HMS).

She was built at Southampton in 1418 by Robert Berd to the design of John Hoggekyns and should not be confused with a later fifteenth century King's ship of the same name or with Henry VIII's *Henri Grace à Dieu*, otherwise known as the *Great Harry*.

The *Grace Dieu of the Tower* was of about 1,400 tons and clinker built of planks made up of three lesser planks bolted together. She had one great mast and a small foremast. She was by far the largest ship afloat but was never in action.

In July 1434 thirty labourers, headed by one Thomas, were paid 38/6 in all for digging a shallow dock in the mud above Bursledon and hauling the *Grace Dieu* into it. Her great mast had already been removed. There she ended her short life for, during the night of January 7th, 1439, she was destroyed by fire.

Up to the time of Henry V, the English Kings had very few ships of their own. They had relied on 'pressing' merchant ships into service in time of war but Henry V made a real attempt to build up a Royal Navy. He built several new 'great ships' as well as smaller attendant vessels, entrusting their supervision to William Soper of Southampton, Clerk and Governor of the Ships. Soper built at Bursledon in 1436 the 1,000 ton ship *Little Jesus of the Tower*, the first ship for the Royal Navy since the *Grace Dieu* of 1418. She too was clinker-built.

When Henry V died in 1422, Soper, who had advanced some of the money to pay for his ships, was still owed a considerable sum. Economies were necessary so many of the smaller ships were sold, but the larger were retained and brought into the Hamble for safety in case of raids by the French. Soper had fortified the Hamble by building a wooden tower and a spiked pale along the shore and had also built two Naval store-houses there. There was also a chain across the river and upstream of this were laid up the *Grace Dieu*, *Little Jesus*, *Trinity Royal* (540 tons) and the *Holy Ghost* (760 tons) as well as several of the smaller ships. There the *Grace Dieu* was burnt out, the *Little Jesus* given to two members of Cardinal Beaufort's household and towed to Southampton and, of the others, there is no trace.

Luckily Soper kept meticulous accounts which still exist, giving a complete list of all pieces of gear and equipment bought for the *Little Jesus* and what it cost. She had her own dinghy or 'Cokbote' and a compass (which few ships of her day carried), costing sixteen pence for 'j diall et j nedell'. He gives the names of the workmen and their pay and how much was spent on security. Total cost of the *Little Jesus* was £143.6.5¾.

By the 14th century the River was certainly the home port of many ships fit to transport an army to France. Indeed, in 1346, the Hamble River supplied 18 ships with a total crew of 325 men to transport the army to France and the Battle of Crecy, and there must have been as many smaller fishing and trading vessels.

Shallow-draught lighters and barges were able to navigate as far as Botley but sailing vessels such as pinks were not able to get further up than Pinkhaven, several hundred yards below the mill.

Pinks originated before 1500 A.D. and were small tubby seagoing merchant vessels, blunt ended like a Dutch boeier but with a narrow overhanging transom, and were of various rigs. The building of Bursledon Bridge in 1800 put an end to such sailing vessels using the upper reaches of the Hamble.

In Henry VIII's day, Hamble was described as a 'good fisshar town with a haven where yn is a very fair rode for great ships'. But the King's ships were not yet being built on the River Hamble.

Richard Wyatt, a master mariner who was born in 1620, built the *Elizabeth of Hamble* at his yard at Bursledon. She was captured by the Dutch in 1667. He was succeeded by his son William and building continued for various trading ventures, particularly with the West Indies, and for other more local use. In 1691 he obtained orders for ships for the King's Navy and launched the *Devonshire* (80 guns) in 1692 and the *Winchester* the following year. He died of smallpox in 1693 but his widow continued to run the business, launching the 80-gun *Lancaster* in 1694, the *Cumberland* and a smaller ship, the *Seaford*, in 1695. In 1698 the River was one of the areas considered by four commissioners as a possible Naval base. The last of the Wyatts died in 1720 at Bursledon without leaving any male heir.

Five years later, Philemon Ewer took over Wyatt's yard and built small craft for coastal trade and fishing boats. For many years Moody Janverin worked for Ewer and in 1734 Janverin set up as a master-shipwright and settled in Hamble where in 1741 he built Hamble House. Originally this building had a slate roof and parapet, as had the Manor House. The rafters over the main drawing room were fifteen inches deep by four inches with a gap of only six inches between them. Perhaps he built his ships as sturdily. The house was demolished in 1960.

Ships were built in the open where there was firm ground near the water and such sites were not always available. So Janverin built at Lepe and Buckler's Hard as well as at Hamble while Ewer used Cowes to build the 70-gun *Vanguard* in 1748. In 1744 he launched the *Folkland* (48 guns) and *Lizard* (14 guns) at Bursledon and the *Ruby* (80 guns) the following year. It is noticeable that, when a large ship was built, smaller ones were built at the same time so that wood could be used up economically.

Ewer's overseer, a Richard Heather, built two ships, the *Triton* (24 guns) in 1745 and *Assurance* (44 guns), which he launched in 1747 while Ewer launched the *Fox* (24 guns) in 1746 and *Anson* (60 guns) in 1747. The *Anson* was a ship of 1,197 tons. Ewer died in 1750 at the age of only 49. He was followed by his son who built three lighters for Portsmouth Dockyard in 1757.

Janverin meanwhile was repairing and building small craft and supplying timber to Portsmouth Dockyard. In 1745 he launched two 14-gunners, the *Hinchinbroke* and *Badger*. The *Badger* (274 tons) had a gun deck 91 feet long and a beam of 26 feet, 14 guns and 14 swivels and carried a crew of 125. In 1748 followed the *Greenwich* (50 guns) and *Fowey* (28 guns) from Lepe, the *Lively* (438 tons, 24 guns, 108 ft. gundeck, over 30 ft. beam and a crew of 165) from Hamble and the *Griffin* (28 guns) from Bursledon. Janverin died in 1766 and is buried at Hamble.

John Smith, a shipwright from Bursledon, joined Joseph Sibnell, a small boatbuilder of Hamble, and built the 44-gun *Humber* which they launched in 1748. Sibnell continued to build small craft and fishing vessels at Hamble into the 1750's for the Society of Free British Fishery.

With the approach of the Napoleonic Wars, shipbuilding for the Navy increased and the Hamble River came in for its full share of the work. George Parsons started building at Land's End, Bursledon, in 1777 and built many ships: the *Fox* (32 guns) in 1780, the *Quebec* (32 guns) 1781, and re-built the 64-gun *Ardent* in 1782 and the *Phoenix* (36 guns) 1783. The *Elephant* (74 guns, 1,644 tons) was launched in 1786 (her bicentenary was celebrated in 1986 at the Elephant Boatyard at Bursledon) and became Nelson's flagship at Copenhagen (where he put his telescope to his blind eye), and the *Dover* (44 guns) in the same year. Parsons also built East Indiamen and several merchant ships, among them the *George & Robert*, *George & Margaret* and

Cognac, a packet for the French brandy trade, as well as repairing many ships.

With the outbreak of war in 1793, he was busy again with Government contracts and a whole list of ships was launched. In 1793 came *Diligence* (16 guns), 1794 *Galatea* (32 guns), 1797 *Cambrian* (40 guns), 1798 *Penelope* (36 guns), 1800 *Jason*, 1801 *Resistance*, 1804 *Tribune*, 1805 *Apollo*, all of 36 guns; 1807 *Horatio* (38 guns), as well as several smaller vessels and lighters. Parsons then moved to a site at Warsash but the yard at Bursledon was still used under the management of Blake and various partners.

The output from the various yards in the River was staggering: from Bursledon came the 382-ton *Doterel* (18 guns) in 1808, *Trinculo* (another 18-gun ship) in 1809, the *Bold* and the *Borer* in 1812, the *Rippon* (74 guns) also in 1812, and the *Sirius* (38 guns) in 1813; while from Warsash came the *Peruvian* (18 guns) in 1808, *Hotspur* and *Theban* (both 36 guns) in 1810 and *Nymphe* (36 guns) in 1812.

George Parsons died in 1812 but John Parsons and John Rubie built another 36-gunner, the *Laurel*, in 1813 at Warsash.

During the period 1741-1814, 46 Naval ships were launched in the Hamble River. During the same period Southampton produced 47 and Beaulieu 54.

Due to the export of timber from the River, there were fears as early as 1579 that the supply of shipbuilding timber on the Hamble was running low and wood had to be brought from further afield to satisfy civil shipbuilding needs. With the intensive naval building activity during the Napoleonic Wars, there can be little wonder that it was more economical to switch much of the work to Beaulieu and Lepe where there was still ample timber close at hand. Many shipwrights were transferred, using the regular Warsash – Ashlett Ferry to get to work.

All this activity naturally meant plenty of employment and shipwrights went from site to site wherever the work was. Hamble Ferry was kept busy as well as the Warsash to Ashlett one while the ferry at Bursledon was supplemented by a wooden bridge in 1800. This was a toll bridge and in that year the takings were £125 but the company bought out the ferry in 1812 and the following year the takings were £1,205.

Besides the shipwrights and fishermen, many ships were manned by locals. In 1812 there was an account of a vessel returning from Ireland with a cargo of corn and how she was captured by a French privateer who took off her captain and put a prize crew aboard. But as soon as the privateer was over the horizon, the mate, a young man from Hamble, re-took the ship and sailed her to Falmouth.

With the end of the Napoleonic Wars, the Hamble River had no more contracts from the Royal Navy. Some of the yards kept going with repairs to small coastal craft and a new industry – yacht building – but this did not help to any great extent in the problems of unemployment. Few were employed in agriculture, in fact in 1801, out of a population of 327, only 13 were so employed and thirty years later, with the population at 318, those on the land numbered but 12.

It was still the sea which called the majority and by 1842 Hamble supplied the Metropolitan market alone with 90,000 lobsters and crabs. The population of Hamble in earlier days is not certain for it is doubtful whether those who lived afloat were counted. That there were many afloat is certain for the population by 1921 had risen to 851 which included an influx of newcomers in the then growing aircraft industry and, of this total, 207 lived afloat.

Government contracts again came to Hamble during the Second World War and the River was the scene of much activity. The mudland between the Parish and Oyster Hards was filled in with rubble from blitzed Southampton and repair workshops were erected by the Americans for the maintenance of small Naval vessels which could be slipped. The concrete floor of the shed is now used for parking cars.

What few people knew about, however, and those few did not talk about, was the assembly of midget submarines on the Hamble. The forward sections of these 'X' Craft, as they were called, were made by Thornycrofts, the midship sections by Vickers-Armstrong in Barrow and the after end by Brigan & Cowan in Hull. In all, twenty different firms had a hand in their building. In great secrecy, the 50 ft. craft was assembled in a shed at Sarisbury Green, trundled down to the River at Moody's in the dead of night in March 1941 and hidden in a canvas-covered floating shed moored in the River. By October 1941, an old drifter, the *Present Help*, was converted into a parent ship and brought to the Hamble to house the crews.

The first 'X' Craft left the Hamble in June 1942 to test the defences of Portland and the mock attack was considered a success. She returned to the River and was taken by special train, covered with tarpaulins, to Loch Striven in Scotland which became the 'X' Craft base. It was X6 and others which attacked the German battleship *Tirpitz* in 1943 and others were used at Bergen, Singapore and the Far East and off the Normandy beaches.

Lukes' yard was at this period engaged in maintaining the Solent Patrol for the Royal Navy.

With the closure of Fairey Marine works at Hamble Point in 1983 matters looked serious for the boatbuilding industry in Hamble until Cougar Marine, a modest boatbuilding business recently established at Netley by former dinghy sailor Clive Curtis, decided to transfer to the Fairey site. There they built the Atlantic Challenger which all but broke the Atlantic crossing record and, further, proceeded to build a 12 metre yacht to challenge Australia for the America's Cup in 1987. In 1985 this was named *Crusader* by the Princess of Wales, adding yet another Royal name to those who have visited Hamble.

Rubble from blitzed Southampton on Hamble Foreshore, 1942.

American patrol boats up for maintenance at Hamble Hard, 1942.

Yachting

Originally a yacht was a vessel designed for the exclusive purpose of carrying passengers, usually royalty, but later it was used to describe any seagoing vessel used for pleasure.

Yachting, then, was for the rich only and, although several yacht clubs were founded in the first half of the 19th century, Hamble was not one of the main venues. However, many local fishermen managed to get jobs aboard yachts in the summer, reverting to their true trade when the season was over. They were delighted to get yachting jobs where food and conditions were so much better than they were used to on fishing smacks and crabbers.

By 1875 there were, however, a few large yachts moored in the River. The largest, perhaps, was the *Triad* (built in 1909 by Caledon of Dundee) a steam yacht of 1,800 tons. By this time the sport had grown to such an extent that there was a very real need for some control over the conduct of racing and a Yacht Racing Association was formed. The three founders included Captain J.W.S. Hughes who lived in Hamble (at Ferryside and at The Summer House). Captain Hughes had four daughters who were amongst the first lady helmsmen. They raced in the Solent in any weather and did much to popularise the sport and make it fashionable. One daughter married Mr. Joe Shenley, the owner of the *Triad* and some forty other yachts.

The ladies in those days raced even the small boats in long skirts, hats and gloves and even carried parasols.

Gradually the sport spread and included those with small incomes and yachts to match.

In 1889 the Minima Sailing Club was formed in Hamble. Its objects were 'to encourage the building, improvement and sailing of small boats and to promote seamanship and sport amongst amateur boat-sailers and also to form branches or out-stations with similar objects'. A clubhouse was built in 1891 on Hamble Point and races were started and finished there. In those days, the annual subscription was half a guinea and members owned two 2½-raters, 12 one-raters and nine half-raters. Branches were started at many places but today the only one still in existence is on the Thames. Their activities at Hamble were halted by the First World War.

Mrs. Shenley in yachting rig of the day about 1905.

After the war, seven local men met on the Village Green and the Hamble River Sailing Club was formed. The first races were held in August 1919. There was no clubhouse, just a wooden hut in the garden of the Bugle Inn to house the Race Officer and his crew and equipment. The annual subscription

Triad moored opposite the Rising Sun at Warsash.

Early stalwarts of Hamble River Sailing Club, l to r: Captain A.A. Walker, Gregory Robinson, Bob Unwin, Harry Barnes, F.D. Hobbs, Walter Luke, about 1930.

'Uncle Bob' Williams about to fire the starting gun, about 1925.

Foreshore and Hamble River Sailing Club, 1930.

was a modest 7/6 and in 1925 those under 21 years of age were encouraged to join at a shilling a year.

The objects of the Club were 'to encourage the sport of small boat sailing and racing' and it saw to it that no keen adherent was excluded for want of funds. Races were arranged twice a week throughout the summer and in 1928 a clubhouse was built, again in the grounds of the Bugle.

The first commodore was Captain Basil Lubbock, author of 'Round the Horn before the Mast', recording his experiences returning from the Gold Rush in Alaska, and many books on the sailing clippers. It was he who built Mere House. He was succeeded by Captain Maurice Henry Horatio Nelson, a lateral descendant of the famous Admiral, and who lived in the Summer House.

In those early years it was not customary to have any additional buoyancy in the dinghies – some even had pigs of ballast – and much seamanship was required not to take too much water aboard. The dinghies were kept on courses in the River itself but this was no great restriction for there was plenty of room in the then uncrowded River. Uncrowded, that is, on the lower reaches. Upstream there were hundreds of wartime MLs (motor launches) laid up in the River as the King's ships had been centuries before. It was not long, however, before the Club insisted on extra buoyancy tanks being tied into the boats and gradually these precautions made it safe enough to sail further into broken water.

Keeled classes racing with the Club included the 'X' Class from 1921 (this is now, in 1987, the biggest single class racing

with the Club), the Sunbeams (which had their first race in May 1923), the old Hamble One Designs, the 'Q' Class and many others.

The Luke family came originally from Limehouse where they had been boatbuilders since 1829. Walter Luke, the eldest of nine children, was born at Limehouse but the rest were born at Itchen Ferry, after the family moved there in 1868. The two brothers, Walter and Albert, started business at a site at Hamble Point in 1895. They built yachts and other small craft for some years and then became involved in making seaplanes but this business failed and the firm went into liquidation just before the war, only to start again in 1914, building aircraft components. At the end of the war they again concentrated on yacht building, having moved to a site upriver just north of the present Royal Southern Yacht Club. Here they stayed, gradually expanding northward, until 1939.

By today's standards, their rather rickety staging and pontoons were primitive but there was nothing haphazard about the yachts they built and repaired. They became a household name among yachtsmen and vessels came from far and near to lay up, either ashore or in mudberths, for the winter. The Luke brothers always managed to find some employment for locals who fell on hard times. The Lukes turned a blind eye to the fact that the firm's time and materials were used to make floats for the annual regatta. Bert Luke was the first Hon. Secretary of Hamble River Sailing Club while his brother Walter later became the Hon. Treasurer and subsequently a Flag Officer.

Hamble Stars and 14 ft. CRCs racing in the River about 1947.

A sailing club, the Upper Hamble Sailing Club, was started upriver but did not flourish. It was wound up during the 1939-45 war and did not reopen.

Between the wars, more and more fishermen found jobs as skippers or hands on the yachts, both large and small. In fact, nearly every racing yacht of six metres or more had a professional hand, and less and less fishing was done. Races were held somewhere in the Solent every weekday but only for a far shorter season than nowadays.

The Second World War brought all yachting to a halt. Amateur yachtsmen and professionals alike were called up, many going into the R.N.V.R. for service in MTBs and minesweepers where their skills were put to good use.

As the sport got going again after the war, it was evident that there had been a great change. The yachts were smaller, there was a great increase in the number of dinghy classes and such was the desire for everybody to get afloat that amateur crews manned almost every vessel. The professionals on the River, who had numbered well over 100, dwindled to only 16 and these were mainly stewards or engineers on the bigger motor yachts.

In 1936 the Royal Southern Yacht Club, which was founded in 1837, found that their premises near the Southampton Town Quay were too hemmed in by the new Docks and they moved to Hamble where they acquired the four cottages on the Quay.

The Hamble River Sailing Club's lease ran out in 1949 and a new clubhouse was built by the Ferry Hard.

The Royal Air Force Yacht Club transferred from Calshot to premises at Riverside House at the end of Rope Walk in 1951.

The Royal Thames Yacht Club took premises at Warsash in 1946 and this clubhouse was also used by the Household Division Yacht Club but Shore House was acquired in 1979 by Warsash Sailing Club which had been formed in 1957.

The yachting boom was on. The moorings became more and more crowded. Swinging moorings almost ceased to exist, the boats being tied fore-and-aft to piles, in many cases two or even five abreast, and marinas for hundreds of boats sprang up in the River. In order to crowd in even more boats, pontoons are now becoming commonplace. Some 200 dinghies are parked on the foreshore at Hamble which had been built up with Southampton's air raid rubble. The whole area between the Quay and the Ferry Hard had until then been mud and sedge.

The reason for the Hamble River's popularity is the same as it always was: double tides, sheltered moorings, the ability to use the River at all states of the tide, no bar at the River mouth, added to which is its geographical position, being now within easy reach of London and the Midlands. All this giving access to some of the finest and most interesting sailing waters in the country, it follows that great pressure is put upon the village and River to accommodate an ever-increasing volume of traffic. With nearly 3,000 craft already using its narrow channel, there is a real danger that it will cease to be a recreational centre because of overcrowding.

Local waters and conditions provide almost every variety of sailing problem: tides, rough and smooth water, confined room in which to manoeuvre, windshifts and plenty of competition and

X Boats and Hamble ODs racing in Hamble River about 1922.

there can be little wonder that the standard of helmsmanship is high amongst those who have served their apprenticeship in such waters. Local clubs have produced National champions in many classes and in 1972 Hamble River Sailing Club had six of their members sailing for Great Britain in the Olympic Games. Several of the old 'J' Class yachts have been laid up in mudberths in the River.

With the tremendous increase in use of the local waters, particularly by those unused to the ways of the sea, it became expedient to have a local inshore rescue boat in the area and such a service was started in 1969, a 35-knot dory, *St. Andrew*, supported by voluntary contributions. It was first based on the Southampton Water shore but is now at Hamble Hard. It was superseded in 1973 by a new and larger launch and in August 1981 by a third, all named after the Patron Saint of Hamble – and of fishermen.

Sailing, by its very nature, attracts the individualist, the loner, the eccentric and the village has had its share of such people for the Hamble is a Mecca to yachtsmen and sooner or later they all 'blow in' or start their world voyages or adventures here.

Admiral Fullerton, captain of the Royal Yacht *Victoria and Albert* for seventeen years, lived in The Cottage (the Cottage was a modest misnomer for the elegant 22-roomed house transformed in the '60s into three sizeable houses. The grounds now also contain the River Green estate) in School Lane, and was frequently visited by Royalty, Mr. 'Curly' Bevis being engaged as pilot whenever the vessel visited Hamble.

In 1873 Mr. Luke built at Itchen Ferry a 75-foot Lifeship to a design by Captain Hans Busk. She was designed specifically for saving life in cases of shipwreck and could be sailed or rowed. Nor were Mr. Luke's sons, building at Hamble, afraid to tackle unusual jobs. One such was a motor boat with a revolving bow to draw the boat along instead of pushing her. She was not a success.

Lukes' experimental motor launch on the Quay.

Regatta

When did village regattas start? What is their origin? In a newspaper report of Hamble Regatta in 1870, the event was described as 'one of the best ever held' and the fireworks were said to be 'wonderful'. The report implies that it was by no means the first.

Certainly the first village regattas were held in the early autumn, usually in September, for they relied largely on the fishermen for active support and it was then that they came up for a scrub and overhauled their gear ready for the winter.

Sailing by coloured searchlights, about 1970.

Hamble Flower Show, 1925. The Hon. Mrs. Eliot Yorke (centre in black coat) and villagers.

Financial support came from the gentry and those who liked to be considered such. The prize money was well worth the effort of dumping all the heavy fishing gear ashore and the fishing boat sailing races were the important events of the day and were contested without too much regard for rules. Prize money, even in a village regatta in the 1870s, amounted to ten or fifteen guineas for first prize and was shared among the professional crew, so competition was keen.

Handicapping was not based on the sophisticated rating of later years. In 1876, the year after the YRA (now the RYA) was founded, an allowance of 80 seconds a ton was given for yachts in the over 15-ton class while, in the 10 to 15-ton class, the allowance was one minute a ton but no length of course was stipulated. That year's race was won by the 20-ton *Vanessa* with an elapsed time of over five hours in 'a capital breeze'. One competitor lost her bowsprit and topmast in a 'strong puff' so it would appear to have been a fairly long course. Years later, handicaps were based on two minutes a foot of waterline length on an eight-mile course.

Prizes for boats under 23 feet, the smallest boats for which there was a race, were £5, £3 and £2. Rowing races, usually in Excise cutters, brought keen rivalry but, once it was over, everything became light-hearted and beer flowed freely as the prize money was spent.

As the yachts became more numerous, sailing races were provided for them in various classes but the main fun was the rowing and aquatic sports which spectators could enjoy, and people came from far and wide to see how the locals disported themselves – approved and often joined in.

Since earliest times, it has been the custom to celebrate the gathering-in of the harvest, an operation helped by almost every available hand, including the children, and followed by a village party. As the scythes gave way to the combine harvesters, the work no longer needed great numbers – just a man and a tractor and a helper or two – no basis for a party.

The void left by such progress seems to have been filled by a sports day and flower show and, in Hamble, this was held either on Mr. Bartlett's field next to Manor Farm or on the Village Green and held in conjunction with the Regatta. Everyone made great efforts to make the day a success and hardly a house was left undecorated by the occupant.

By the mid-1920s, the income came almost entirely from yachtsmen and the cost of running a flower show and land sports became somewhat of a burden to the Regatta funds. Reluctantly both flower show and sports ceased to function.

But a village, if it is to maintain its character, must let its hair down once a year so great efforts were made to build up first a water carnival and later a land carnival and procession. During

the 1930s, this side of the festivities grew and developed into one of the best in the country, maintaining a spirit of co-operation which is often lacking in larger communities, and still people come from far and wide to see and enjoy one of the local traditions.

The fireworks which traditionally brought the Saturday events to a close were an attraction until the 1980s when rising costs and dangerous congestion of yachts near the shore made this unwise. Another great crowd-puller was the innovation of formation sailing by the light of coloured searchlights in the 1960s. These activities, however, have had to be curtailed owing to the immense increase in river traffic and the consequent number of piles and moorings.

Above: The Victory Inn decorated for Regatta Day 1930.

Left: Carnival Procession arrives at the Quay on Regatta Day, about 1932.

The Quay, about 1905.

Regatta 1929 with decorated floats.

JAMES AYLING, Shell Fish Merchant, HAMBLE.
Fishmongers supplied with LOBSTERS, CRABS & CRAW-FISH,
With despatch, to all parts of the country. A constant supply of
OYSTERS WHEN IN SEASON.

The Quay about 1860.

The Quay

From records of the Admiralty Court of 1566 we learn that 'the Kaye of Hamble is in decaye' and instructions were given for its repair. It seems that time has now disposed of all trace of the original structure.

The Royal Southern Yacht Club occupies the four cottages on the Quay as well as two on the corner of Rope Walk and they have acquired the adjoining land as far as Riverside House. The four on the Quay were built in 1819 and were, from the River end, Quay House, Rose Cottage, Magnolia Cottage and Sundial Cottage.

Quay House was at one time a beer house under the command of Ann Bullmore. It is not clear how long this was so

Foreshore and Quay, 1907.

Crabber and Ferryside Cottage, 1910.

Spring tide on the Foreshore, 1930.

A view from the Bugle in 1905.

but from 1855 to 1859 it was so recorded and was remembered as a 'bough house' by old men living in the 1920s, 'bough' or bush being the sign of a tavern. hence the expression 'good wine needs no bush'.

About this time, one upstairs room was used as a school by Mr. Bryer. The premises were used around the turn of the century as a repository by Whites of Southsea and also for storing fishing gear, nets, trawls, etc., until it was bought in 1908 by the artist Gregory Robinson. He and some companions were arrested as spies in 1912 when cruising in the yacht *Silver Crescent* off the coast of Germany. He 'just happened' to be sketching the defences of the Kiel Canal but all were released after nine days in prison and much string-pulling and newspaper headlines.

Some years earlier Erskine Childers in the *Dulcibella* cruised in the same area and subsequently wrote 'The Riddle of the Sands', exposing a German plan to invade the East Coast. The *Dulcibella* lay in the Hamble for some years. After Gregory Robinson moved to Satchell Lane in 1926, Quay House became a teashop serving Hamble's well-known crab teas.

The magnolia tree was planted by a Mrs. Ponsford when she was 12 years old. That was in 1880. It was a cutting given her by the gardener at Ferryside, Jim Russell, who later became the Hamble boatman.

Old engravings show the Quay at which crabs and fish, and probably other goods as well, were unloaded. Crab boxes on wheels could be run into the water to keep the crabs alive and pulled ashore when needed. There was an old tree in the middle of the Quay on a branch of which the catches were weighed, but in March 1871 it broke, killing Robert Scovell, the owner of many of the crabbers. After such a tragedy, of course, the tree was cut down.

By 1920 only a few stumps showed where the Quay had been.

Silver Crescent off Kiel shortly before her crew were arrested as spies, 1912.

On the south side, at the bottom of the High Street, there used to be an old timbered house which was occupied by generations of the Penny family. It was pulled down in 1910 and Riverbank built on the site. In 1986 Riverbank was converted into two flats with an unrivalled view of the River.

Also facing the water is Leonard House, now a restaurant, which is at least a hundred years older than Quay House. The holder of the deeds was entitled to a pew in the church.

Above: Riverbank and the Bugle about 1900.

Left: Leonard House, the Quay.

Buildings

The activities of the Church, nobility and Lords of the Manor have been reasonably well documented throughout the ages but of simple village life little was written at the time and conjecture has had to play too large a part. In Hamble there has been no resident Lord of the Manor: this position has been occupied by Winchester College since 1391 although in 1859 Thomas Chamberlayne, who lived at Botley, was described as 'Lord of the Manor of Hamble'.

Little is known of the old cottages in and around Hamble except what is shown on the few large-scale early maps. From these we know only of their existence at certain dates. Stories of those who lived in them have been handed down to us but little can be learnt from the few records that still exist.

Shepherds and carters lived in some small two-roomed cottages in Satchell Lane; shipwrights, rope-makers, mariners and other tradesmen lived in the Square, in High Street and Rope Walk (originally Back Street) where there was also a chapel. The cottages around the Square have stood for many a century and the Olde House used to be three cottages until they were knocked into one in about 1910. These date from the 13th century and, with rooms clustered around great central fireplaces and the fine timber and herring-bone brick exterior, it is an excellent example of the architecture of that period.

Coppers for boiling tar for the treatment of ropes and other nautical requirements stood where Copperhill Terrace now stands.

Below: The Olde House, about 1900.
Above: The Olde House in 1930 as one unit.

46

Copperhill Terrace in the 1970s.

A view of Ferry Lane from Hamble Green.

Ye Olde Whyte Harte and bakehouse, 1905.

Ferryside Cottage, 1930.

Purbrook Cottages in the High Street were picturesque thatched homes until the early years of this century. Parts of the Bugle Inn, formerly known as The Ferry House, are probably 13th century. Manor Cottages and many other buildings are known to be extremely old, as is Portland House, another case of three cottages being knocked into one. The Olde Whyte Harte, the Gun House and Ferryside Cottages still stand while other newer buildings are built on foundations of great antiquity. The village smithy beside the Olde House has been replaced by a bank.

Of the larger and more modern houses, and of their inhabitants, more is known.

The building of Sydney Lodge was started in 1789 by Captain Sir Joseph Sydney Yorke but it was some years before it was completed, much of the cost being met out of prize money awarded to the Captain for capturing French Men-of-War during the Napoleonic Wars. The house was designed by Sir John Soane and was noted for its great staircase and hall. Captain Yorke's son, the fourth Earl of Hardwicke, was born at Hamble in 1799 and rose to the rank of Admiral. He was Lord Lieutenant of Cambridgeshire, became Postmaster General in 1852 and later Lord Privy Seal. Sydney Lodge is now occupied by British Aerospace.

On Westfield Common, now sadly in a dilapidated state, is a saluting base built by Captain Yorke to salute ships arriving in

the Roads off his estate. The base contained six cannon which he had brought home from a Dutch frigate, the *Alliance*, which he had captured in 1805. Captain Yorke was drowned in 1831 and a tablet was set in the parapet in his memory by the fourth Earl in 1871. The base was kept in good repair until 1931 when the estate was sold and the guns taken to the family seat in Gloucester where they were probably melted down for munitions in the last war.

Hamble Cliffe House close by was built in 1809 and some of its windows have tracery under four central arches which probably came from Netley Abbey.

The twenty-two roomed 'Cottage' in School Lane (at one time the home of Admiral Sir John Fullerton), was later that of Lady Helena Best (Lady Helena was the daughter of the Hon. Victor Montagu, heir to the Earl of Sandwich, and Lady Agneta Helena Yorke, daughter of the 4th Earl of Hardwicke. Her father died before he could succeed to the Earldom and his daughter was given the title of 'Lady' by Special Remainder). Many village fêtes were held in the grounds under a magnificent beech tree and an adjoining field of daffodils was one of the sights of the village in the springtime and furnished many generations of children with posies for Mothering Sunday.

A photograph taken in 1905 from Hamble Common shows the Common Pond and in the distance can be seen the Church. This was, of course, before 'The Copse' was built and the

The Copse, demolished 1985.

The Cottage, School Lane, and weeping ash.

Hamble House, demolished 1960.

Riverside House, 1868.

Ravenswood, demolished 1930 and replaced by Crowsport Estate.

Grantham Lodge, destroyed by Second World War bomb.

All that remains of Ravenswood, probably the icehouse.

strange building to find in a simple old village. The family very generously helped many local causes including the school, Memorial Hall and the local Sea Rangers. When the last of the Emmons family finally left the village, the estate was sold for development and at the time of writing several large modern houses have been built and a road cut through from Shell Mex Road to School Lane.

Hamble Manor House was built in the latter half of the 18th century and, there being no resident lord of the Manor, was called Hamble Green House until after the First World War. It used to have a fine uninterrupted view over Southampton Water, as there was a ha-ha on the south side of the Green, that is a wall hidden in a ditch with meadows beyond. For a short while it was a hotel and is now a block of flats.

There is now no trace of Hamble House which had been built by the shipbuilder Janverin in 1740 and much later became the home of Sir Alliott Verdon Roe. It was pulled down in 1960 and replaced by a modern house where lived the Principal of the Air College till 1983.

Another large house which is no longer part of the Hamble scene was Ravenswood. This was demolished and Crowsport estate built in its place. This rather sombre building was surrounded by a high stone wall. The only traces of the former house is an east-facing doorway, probably originally leading to an ice house.

The Summer House, now in the grounds of the College of Air Training and about to be demolished, was built by the well-known yachtsman, Mr. Fred Hughes, and later became the home of Captain Maurice Henry Horatio Nelson.

The Vicarage, originally the Rectory, dates from 1821 and was built with money from Queen Anne's Bounty. It has now been superseded by a modern vicarage, facing the High Street, and has been turned into a private house, renamed Dulcars, the name of the field on which it was built.

ornamental trees planted. Mr. Van Buren Emmons came to live in Hamble at the turn of the century with his wife, the grand-daughter of Martin Van Buren who was President of the United States of America from 1837 to 1841, and The Copse was built in magnificent style with lofty rooms and elegant staircases. A

The Village Green and Manor Cottages.

Tea party under the beech tree, The Cottage, School Lane.

Copperhill Terrace from the Square, 1905.

Village Life

The Coffee Rooms in Rope Walk were built by the Hon. Mrs. Eliot Yorke as a home for the old folk and the many widows of the village and she put it in the care of one of her former maids, a Mrs. Woods. Her daughter, Mary Jane, was born there in 1868, living there until she was married and moved, as Mrs. Ponsford, to Netley. From her letters we get an insight into village life when she was young.

'When the Mercury came and built the House in Satchell, no houses after Copperhill Terrace, but a few farmers cottages and Windsors Mansion [Ravenswood] . . . an old farm and pond and a Daffodil Field in which a terrace [Daffodil Terrace] is now built. Well Lane, the pump we all had to get our water from for washing and all so we were careful of rainwater.

My stepfather rowed the ferry for years. The old chapel was still there . . . a Mr. Elsie, gardener at Hamble House, preached there . . . There were tea fights as we called them and people used to come and have a nice time. There was a bank opposite we used to play on and a garden used to belong to the Scovels we used to get into the Goose B also a garden opposite us belonged to the Taylors with apple trees . . . a little shipyard was next to the coal yard, the yacht men filled their barrels at the well in the coal yard opposite our house, we got water often there. The House next the chapel was a grand house once, Miss Bradbury lived there and there was a great kitchen and a wide oak stairs but those days passed. Two sisters lived each side, one a widow Mrs. Dove took in washing and mending for a living, her husband was drowned in the river as so many more were in the smacks, never came back from the North Sea spratters.

The tide used to come up Spring Tides and go into several houses and my brother rowed us along the street in a boat to school.

On Bank Holiday Whit, Hamble Club used to have a dinner at the Victory where the Vicar and other gentlemen presided they gave donations generally £5 for the year then they all walked to Sidney Lodge to play, also to Church. Then we all went round the Green to listen to the Band and beer also was taken round. All had a good time till the Band went back over the water to Fareham. The children at the School, Mr. Canceller Vicar gave a treat every year, also the parents in the evening in the field near the Vicarage, also the Girl Friendly Society which I belonged. You had to be good and get a certificate and Bible which I and my sister both received. On Good Friday we took primroses to Church, we received an orange and bun most gratefully.

I remember all the Royalty at the funeral of Mrs. Hon. Alex Yorke and also Mr. Elliot and Lady Hardwick where I lived as nurse to her Grand L. She laid in state. I left in 1886 went and work to Ad. Fullerton as childrens maid.'

It was a hard life but they had their fun. At the age of 94, she added a point which had perhaps rubbed off from her service with the gentry: 'P.S. Please excuse paper I can't find the match to envelope.'

Life was not such a rush, there was time to play cricket in the street or parade round the village with garlands on poles singing:

'First of May is Garland Day,
Chimney Sweeper's Holiday.'

Time, too, just to sit and wait for the tide.

The Gun House, Olde Whyte Harte and Bakery, about 1905.

The Band of Hope outside the Bugle, c. 1880.

Children in the Square on 'Garland Day' (1st May).

Defence

What few remains there are of St. Andrew's Castle can still be seen on the Southampton Water shore of Hamble Common. Sir William Paulet, who later became the Marquess of Winchester, was commanded by Henry VIII to build a number of forts for the defence of Southampton and Portsmouth. Twelve such forts were built, at Hurst, Southsea, Calshot, Hamble and Netley and at Cowes and other places on the Isle of Wight.

St. Andrew's was built in about 1542 with stone from Beaulieu Abbey and from the refectory of Netley Abbey. Both these Abbeys had been abolished in 1535 although Netley remained roofed until 1700.

Hamble Castle had square ends but may have been rounded on the seaward side and probably, like Netley Castle, had firing positions on the parapet as well as below. It was armed with culverines of 5½-inch calibre and sakers of 3-inch calibre and had a range of about 1,000-2,000 yards. There was a moat on the landward side but this has become filled with shingle and is now almost obliterated.

In 1642 the Captain of the Castle was paid 1s 8d per week, an Under Captain 10d, five men at 8d and eight gunners at 6d, making a total cost of £85.3.4. a year. By comparison, Calshot Castle cost £107 a year.

In the mud to seaward of the stone castle there is a pattern of wooden stakes which appear to be earlier defence works or to prevent erosion.

When the Castle fell into disuse, most of the stones were spirited away to form various walls around the village and the remainder have been moved by erosion, leaving little evidence of its former size and shape. Nearby is a more recent gunsite and a mound in which explosives were kept by the Volunteers of the last century.

The Volunteer Movement in the country started when a Charter was granted by Henry VIII in 1537 to the 'Masters and Rulers of the Science of Artillery for cross-bows and band guns'. That original Volunteer Corps is now the Honourable Artillery Company of London. It was not until 1779 that the Volunteers became an integral part of our national defence.

In 1803 England declared war on France and Napoleon gathered his forces at Boulogne, intending to invade but, in a few weeks, 300,000 Volunteers enrolled and armed themselves at their own expense. After the Napoleonic Wars, the force was gradually reduced to 30,000, only to receive a new impetus in 1859. It was then that the 1st Hampshire Artillery Volunteers were officially recognized, being only the second Volunteer Corps in Great Britain. Its function was to man the defences of Portsmouth and Southampton Water.

The original drill and practice battery was on Hamble Common from which the first salute was fired in 1863. In 1866, the Corps had two field guns (brass nine-pounders) and an eight-inch iron mortar at Hamble. From 1869 to 1879 the Hamble Battery consisted of two 24-pounders and, from 1880 to 1891, two 64-pounder guns.

In 1879 the bursting of a gun in a competition at Hamble resulted in several men being injured, one, Gunner F. Burch, being detained at Netley Hospital with a broken leg. He was subsequently granted a life pension of one shilling per day and was the first Volunteer ever to receive a pension.

In Hampshire in 1801, there were 1,500 infantry Volunteers, 1,200 cavalry and 800 artillery. The man in charge of the Hamble Battery and one of the most ardent Volunteers was Augustus Hooker of the Olde Whyte Harte who was photographed standing beside the exploded gun.

Augustus Hooker and the exploded cannon on Hamble Common, 1880.

First World War Patrol Boats laid up five abreast stretching from Hamble to Bursledon.

For gun drill at Hamble men were conveyed by horse brake to the Common and, after practice, sufficient time was allowed for the popular crab tea.

The Volunteer Movement was brought to an end in 1908 and was replaced by the Territorial Force.

Many cannon balls have been found on Hamble Point. Some had probably been fired from the Volunteers' battery. These are mostly about 8-inch diameter and weigh 45 lb., being hollow and packed with explosive. They are fitted with a wooden time fuse and were made between 1820 and 1830. The area is also sprinkled with fragments of those which exploded. They were probably the first experimental 'shells'.

Several 5½-inch and 3-inch cannon balls have also been found in the mud off Hamble Spit.

There were surprisingly few air attacks made on Hamble during the 1939-45 war – just the odd stick of bombs and a few mines which were probably meant for the shipping channel in Southampton Water. A Heinkel bomber dropped four bombs, one of which destroyed Grantham Cottage, but it was brought down by a Dutch destroyer refuelling at Shell's jetty.

In the early days, a Messerschmidt once joined A.S.T. pupils on their training circuit but flew off without any warlike action so in 1940 the Flying School was moved to Watchfield, near Swindon, and training continued with fewer interruptions to flying schedules. One morning a Junkers machine-gunned a hangar, causing one death, and one night a few incendiaries fell on the airfield.

The main air defence in the area was a large battery at Grange Lane, Netley, but there was a Bofors anti-aircraft gun on the Hamble aerodrome and a Naval gun on the railway was sometimes in the area. There was also a gunsite on Hamble Common and numerous anti-invasion pill-boxes in the area.

Battleship Mast

This mast was erected near the entrance to Badnam Creek at the instigation of Commander Smith-Cumming in 1910 when he was in command of the Boom Defence of Southampton Water. There were two dolphins (groups of posts to secure hawsers) on the Hook shore and six old gunboats and sloops were kept ready off Badnam. They were to have been joined together with wires and nets and booms for defence against torpedo and submarine attack should there be a war.

The mast was brought round from Portsmouth. It had been the mainmast of *HMS Sultan*, one of the Royal Navy's first ironclads of 9,290 tons and 12 guns, built at Chatham in 1868, launched in 1870 and commissioned by Capt. E.W. Vansitart in 1871 for the Channel Squadron. She was recommissioned at Portsmouth for the Mediterranean Fleet in 1876 by the then Duke of Edinburgh. In 1878 she was again recommissioned at Malta and in 1882 took part in the bombardment of Alexandria. In 1889 she struck a rock in the Comino Channel, Sardinia, and sank. She was salvaged and reconstructed during 1891-2 and placed on reserve at Portsmouth until 1906 when she was renamed *Fisgard IV* and used by the Navy for a further 28 years. In 1946 her hulk was handed over to the British Iron & Steel Corporation for breaking.

The Admiral Class were, fortunately most people thought, never in battle. They were designed with the theory that action would be fought end on so the transverse bulkheads of the central battery were of thick armour with practically none at the sides.

The mast at Hamble consisted of a military top and the crowsnest. The military top contained machine guns and searchlights. As it happened, the Boom Defence was placed out

Boom Defence Vessels by the Battleship Mast before the First World War, also showing *T.S. Mercury* and steam yacht *Triad*.

by Horse Sand Fort at the eastern end of Spithead and across the Needles Channel during the 1914-18 war.

The mast was used by Southampton Harbour Board as a Hydrographic Survey Mark. When erected, it went 30 feet into the mud before hitting hard sand and, when the mud was bucketed out, that part filled after a few days with fresh spring water which was used for drinking by the Boom Defence crews.

The mast became dangerous and was taken down in 1956.

Soon after the Armistice in 1918, the Navy's Boom Defence headquarters were set up at Gosport. They took from Hamble the old name *HMS Sultan*.

The Battleship Mast and Derrick at the mouth of Badnam Creek.

Village Schools and the T.S. Mercury

In 1815 a piece of land known as Little Marsh had been given to John Sparshott, together with the brewhouse in School Lane. This seems to be the first reference to a school in Hamble. It would be pointless on this evidence, however, to look for a brewhouse in what is now School Lane. The one at the Gun House was dated 1817 (mason's mark R.A.). The village school in that Lane was not built until 1841 and there had not been one on its site before.

The tithe map of 1837 shows No. 1 Copperhill Terrace as being a school and as being occupied by one Charles Roach who

Hamble School about 1900.

was presumably the schoolmaster. It is not clear if this had been so in 1815 or which was then School Lane.

In 1795 the population of Hamble was 293 of whom 126 were children and, although of course these would not all have been of school age, there must have been many in need of education who did not get any academic instruction.

The building of a Church school in 1841 for the sum of £410 must have been quite an event. It was built on land provided by Winchester College and included a schoolmaster's house. The Vicar was sole manager of the School and appointed the schoolmaster who had one assistant. The school was financed from pupils' fees, the revenue from the rent of Henville House, which was built in 1845 (Charles Henville was Vicar from 1838 to 1850) and donations from local wealthy residents. As a Church school, Hamble was not subject to inspection other than by the Vicar, which he did daily. By 1880 there were 80 pupils.

The Education Act of 1891 brought free education but the then Vicar, the Rev. J.H. Cancellor, asked parents to continue to make subscriptions in lieu of fees to the tune of 5/- or 10/- a year. In the following years, a quarter of the school's income still came from this source. £300 was spent in 1892 on the provision of a further classroom to accommodate the extra children, when the leaving age was raised to eleven. In that year, too, the school had its first inspection by H.M. Inspector who reported that 'the school was doing good work', and this continued for the rest of the century, teaching Scripture and the three R's with drawing for boys and needlework for girls.

During the First World War there were many extra pupils as children of the staff at Netley Military Hospital came to Hamble school and the older children had only part-time education because of accommodation problems.

A further classroom was added in 1928 but, with the rapid growth of the village's industries, by 1937 it was necessary to build another school in Satchell Lane and the old school became a Primary school only. The Senior school has had to have many extensions since it was built to accommodate a rise from 242 pupils in 1937 to 636 in 1967. In 1953 a new Primary school was opened in Hamble Lane by the Duke of Wellington, Lord Lieutenant of Hampshire, leaving about 150 infants at the original school. In 1978, however, the school was forced to close, the remaining infants going to the Primary school. The old school building has since been attractively transformed into three houses with little alteration to the external aspect.

While all this was going on, the children of those who could afford it received private education and, for a time, there was another school whose master was a Mr. Bryer. This man had been born in 1793 at Pear Tree Green and spent much time at sea as a navigator and, when discharged due to injuries, became the Hamble postman. He collected the mail at Woolston and walked to Hamble where, after delivering it, he took classes in an upstairs room at Quay House (now part of the Royal Southern Yacht Club). There he taught mathematics and navigation to those who needed it – mainly skippers of fishing smacks and crabbers. He then collected the outgoing mail and walked back to Woolston.

One morning he was stopped on the road by a gentleman who wished to see what mail he carried but he steadfastly refused the request. 'But,' said the gentleman, 'I am the Postmaster General'. It was no good: old Bryer refused to deliver up the mail except at the correct addresses. 'I wouldn't give them up on the road, not for the Queen of England herself', he said. The gentleman, though, *was* the Postmaster General, the Earl of Hardwicke, who lived at Sydney Lodge close by, and the postman was dubbed 'an honest man' and granted a special pension. This was about 1852 and he continued his little school for several more years. He owned a vessel named *Liberty*.

Mr. Bryer – 'an honest man'.

Before 1885 there were two ways of getting into the Royal Navy: by paying fees and training as officers or by being sent to a reformatory or orphanage and getting trained free. There was no way for an honest but poor boy to get sea training. He would have left school at the age of 11 and was not eligible for the Royal Navy until he was 15.

To remedy this sad state of affairs Charles Hoare, the banker, bought the barque *Illova* and renamed her *Mercury*. This vessel was originally ship-rigged and had been built in Aberdeen and named after a river in South Africa. With the *Pantomime* (153 tons), *Thalia* (13 tons) and *Whisper* (17 tons), free or nearly free sea training was provided for over 100 boys. *Illova* was moored at Binstead in the Isle of Wight and kept in a seagoing condition. In 1888 she cruised to the Mediterranean with 132 boys and 20 seamen. After training most boys joined the Royal or Merchant Navies and glad those services were to accept such trained recruits.

In 1892 the ship was moved to the Hamble River and moored off Mr. Hoare's house, built the previous year, buildings were erected and the boys spent more time ashore in classrooms and at drill. Sixteen years later Charles Hoare died and, as there was no endowment and no money left to run the ship, it seemed that the establishment must close.

Luckily his friend, C.B. Fry, the scholar who represented his country at cricket, athletics and football and obviously had a brilliant career before him, was so annoyed 'at the sheer stupidity of allowing such a work to die', that he put other things aside and carried it on. Sufficient money was raised by the Frys' many friends and, in 1909, a Scheme of Management was approved. With 'C.B.'s popularity and the drive and devotion of his wife Beatrice, whom he married in 1898, the school continued, although money was never plentiful. Mrs. Fry sold her pearls to pay for the theatre (Clara Butt, the famous prima donna, once sang there) in the grounds, which was a scaled down replica of the Wagner Theatre at Bayreuth which had attracted her on a visit to Germany.

The School, Hamble after extensions.

T.S. Mercury, ex-*Illova*, moored near to Mercury House about 1912.

Shore Establishment of *T.S. Mercury*.

C.B. Fry and J.H. Bartlett of Manor Farm in Satchell Lane.

Left: Charles Hoare and W.G. Grace on *T.S. Mercury's* Cricket Pitch.

Top left: Beatrice Fry.

Top right: The Duke of York (later George VI) at the Mercury, accompanied by Mrs. Fry.

In 1914, through the good offices of the First Lord of the Admiralty, Mr. Winston Churchill, the *Mercury* was able to obtain, on permanent loan, *HMS President* (ex-*Gannet*). She was towed from the West India Docks to Hamble just before the war. During the First World War, *Mercury* obtained cash bonuses from the Admiralty for turning out 'advance class boys' but this happy state did not last long. Between the wars it cost about £70 a year to keep a boy and the ship's company mustered up to 150. In 1923 a collection of about 20 ship models in the *Mercury's* museum was sold for about £30,000 (Sir James Caird bought them and presented them to the National Maritime Museum) and this enabled the work to continue.

Music was encouraged and the *Mercury's* Band was in great demand at fêtes and carnivals. Swimming, too, was essential and all boys had to be able to swim at least 1,000 yards before leaving. During the 83 years of rowing over a hundred boys to and from the ship, in all weathers and often in the dark, one boy only was drowned. This was in 1911. Another boy, Maurice Driver, made a determined attempt to avert the tragedy and was subsequently presented with the Albert Medal for bravery.

Smaller auxiliary vessels, the *Vishala* and the *Diana*, were used for practical instruction at sea and made trips to the Mediterranean with 25 boys.

Gradually changes in outlook by education authorities placed more emphasis on academic matters and less on self-discipline, clean and practical living, and the training ship received less and less financial help.

In 1946 Beatrice Fry died after a lifetime of service to the Ship and, in 1950, Commander Fry gave up his post of Honorary Director.

He was succeeded as Captain-Superintendent by Commander Matthew Bradby whose family connections with Hamble can be traced back for two centuries. Under him *Mercury* continued but greater emphasis was put on passing General Certificate of Education examinations than on outdoor activities and seamanship. He was succeeded in 1960 by Cdr. Ronald Hoyle but, despite tremendous efforts to carry on, money was not forthcoming and the School was forced to close in 1968. Many local residents were angry 'at the sheer stupidity of allowing such a work to die'.

The School's chapel, St. Agatha's, was built by Charles Hoare, who was deeply religious, but it was tragically burnt down in 1960. A new chapel, St. Agatha & St. Nicholas, was consecrated in 1962 but removed in 1972. The nearly life-size crucifix which used to hang on the chapel wall, has since been discovered in a derelict condition. The Old Boys' Association had it restored and regilded and, at the celebrations marking the centenary of the foundation of the *Mercury*, this was rededicated and established at the south side of the village church surmounting a stone bearing words of Beatrice Fry:

> Dedicated to minds that can soar, that will rise and not be discouraged by obstacles or difficulties, that will chance and dare for what they love and know to be right.
> To co-operation, combination, dash, perseverance and unselfishness, this TS Mercury and its adjuncts are fearlessly dedicated. For harmony, the good of mankind and to hearts that can beat for others. Its ideal is Good Friday's Hero.

The 25-roomed house, the theatre and other buildings, including the War memorial, were demolished by a developer.

In 1985, as part of the centenary celebrations, a memorial stone was erected by the Old Boys' Association. Buried beneath was a time capsule of letters and pictures. Sir Alec Rose performed the unveiling ceremony. On one side of the stone, which was placed at the end of the creek where the ship would

HMS Gannet, later *HMS President* and *T.S. Mercury* about 1880.

The two Training Ships and the Ship's Company swimming.

have been in view, were the words of Beatrice Fry: '. . . and so she passed into the quiet starlit water of memory and there she will remain until the stars pale in the great dawn which will turn her spars to gold . . . she will lay a course through the islands of the blessed to join company with all good ships in the splendid haven'. The other side bears the ship's motto: 'Men are the Souls of ships'.

The only relics of the training ship to remain in Hamble are the names of those killed in the Great War beside the village memorial in the churchyard; the small terrace in Satchell Lane

T.S. Mercury Ship's Company by the War Memorial in the '30s.

named (now ironically) 'Mercury View'; the newer Mercury Gardens, Fry Close and St. Agatha's Road built on the playing field and the grave of the training establishment; and the Mercury Marina.

The *Illova* was originally ship-rigged 396 tons, built by Alexander Hall of Aberdeen, a famous builder of clipper ships, in 1867 and traded with Africa until bought by Charles Hoare in 1885. For a time both *Illova* and the old *Gannet* lay in the River but in 1916 *Illova* was towed away and became a coaling hulk until lost in a gale in the English Channel.

The *Gannet* was a composite (iron frames, wooden-planked) sloop of 1,124 tons, fitted with a single screw and engine developing 1,110 horse power. She was launched in 1878 and her complement of 118 saw service in the Pacific until 1883. She was recommissioned in 1885 for service in the Mediterranean where she served for ten years, shelling Arab positions in 1888. She returned and was placed in reserve until 1903 when she became HMS *President*, headquarters of the RN Reserve in London, for eight years. She was lent to the *Mercury* in 1914 and remained in the River until 1980 when she was towed away and now lies at the Hardway, Gosport. It is hoped that one day she may be restored to her original rig.

The Scout Movement

It was in June 1907 that General Robert Baden-Powell first took a group of boys to camp on Brownsea Island and, by early 1908, five patrols of Scouts (40 boys) were formed at the *Mercury* under the leadership of the Chaplain, the Rev. Mr. Bloemfeld. 'BP' was a frequent visitor to his friend, C.B. Fry, as was Col. Crichton (Scout Commissioner) who lived at nearby Netley Castle so it is not surprising that Scouting got away to an early start at the *Mercury*.

'BP' asked his brother, Warrington, to draw up rules for Sea Scouts on the lines of those at the *Mercury*. This he did but it was not until July 25th 1910 that the Mercury Troop was registered as the first ever Sea Scouts.

In 1908 there was also formed a patrol of Scouts in Hamble Village but this was not registered at that time as there was no Scout Leader. A troop in the village was registered in 1920 (Scoutmaster Edgar Atkins) but this seems to have closed down for another troop was registered on February 26th 1923 by Scoutmaster Reg Calvert and that troop still flourishes today. Sadly he was murdered by pirates while cruising in the West Indies in the 'seventies.

In April 1910 a Mercury Scout, Enrick by name, jumped overboard and saved another boy who was in imminent danger of drowning. He was subsequently awarded the first Silver Cross in the Scouts.

Other Scouts of the Mercury troop to be honoured were Driver, a Bronze Cross, while Yeatman was awarded a Silver Cross a year later.

66

972 COL CRICHTON PINNING ON MARTIN'S BADGE
T.S. MERCURY, HAMBLE.

Scouts on *T.S. Mercury* Sports Field.

6th Itchen Hamble Sea Scouts, 1938.

Lower High Street and local grocer's shop (now Compass Point) about 1900. Original Post Office is next door.

Fire Brigade

It was normal practice for the Navy to insist on fire fighting precautions being taken at the sites where their ships were being built and so Hamble may have had some fire-fighting arrangements before other villages of its size. The equipment would probably not have amounted to more than a few buckets and some long poles with hooks for pulling down any burning timbered houses to stop the spread of a conflagration.

Subsequently fire brigades were run by insurance companies and they marked the houses for which they were responsible by affixing their plaques to the wall. There were a few premises in Hamble bearing plaques but only that on Portland Cottages (now Portland House) remains. This was issued by the Phoenix Insurance Company which maintained a brigade in Southampton.

Efficient as these brigades were, there were obvious shortcomings and it was not until 1906 that a Hamble Fire Brigade was raised. It consisted of a hand cart, hoses and other equipment costing about £50 and which was paid for by the gentry of Hamble.

Its first home was a small shed opposite The Cottage in School Lane but, when Abbeymead was built, it was moved further along the Lane and kept in a thatch-roofed shed in the grounds of The Copse. The crew of twelve volunteers held frequent practices but it was not until 11th July 1910 that it received its first call – and that turned out to be a case for stretcher bearers and not fire-fighters.

In 1926 there was a fire at the Mercury but Satchell Lane was quite impassable as main drainage was being laid at the time and the truck had to be manhandled across fields, over stiles and barbed wire fences, hedges and ditches – but it got there.

The station was later moved to a site opposite the Memorial Hall where in 1940 up-to-date equipment was installed. This was superseded in 1986 by yet larger premises nearby, accommodating two fire engines.

Railways

Stephenson's Rocket, which got steam up in 1829, was followed by a nationwide Railway Madness and lines shot out in all directions over the country. Even before the London and Southampton Railway was completed in 1840, there were plans for a branch line from Bishopstoke through Botley and Fareham to Gosport. This line was opened on 29th November, 1841, but had to be closed again after four days because the tunnel at Fareham was unsafe. It was reopened in 1842 and some of the grain from Botley Mill and other commodities arrived by rail instead of by boat. At that period, the coke-burning engine used did not appear to be a great advance on the Rocket and the driver always kept to the same engine and had his name exhibited in the cab.

At first, the arrival of the railways had little effect on coastal traffic and the Hamble, with its water-borne connections with the Isle of Wight, the Channel Islands and France, was little affected. Most of the coal supplies for the riverside villages continued to be brought from Sunderland in large coastal vessels to Southampton and thence in sailing barges to Hamble, Warsash, Swanwick and Botley and, so far as Hamble village was concerned, this was the case until about 1920, the barges unloading at Taylor's Wharf.

The foundation stone of the Military Hospital at Netley was laid by Queen Victoria on Whit Monday, 1856, and the Royal Victoria Hospital, as it was named, was completed in 1859. Although the Hospital had its own pier at which casualties from overseas could be disembarked, there was a need for a railway line to serve such a large establishment. The original intention was to build a branch line from Fareham to Netley and thence to Woolston but this was shelved in favour of a line from St. Denys to Netley which was opened in 1866 (5th March). The extension into the Hospital grounds itself was not built until 1900, casualties until then being disentrained in what is now the goods yard. Until 1910, the line and its subsequent extension was single track.

The extension eastward from Netley was in 1862 designed to go through the fields (now the airfield) and cross Satchell Lane about 100 yards north of Satchell Farm and thence over a bridge across the River. This scheme met opposition from the Admiralty who did not savour such an obstruction on the lower reaches of the River.

In the event, the connection with Fareham was diverted upriver through Bursledon and opened in 1889.

Mr. Hoare, who owned the *TS Mercury*, applied for permission to have a narrow-gauge line from Netley Station to the Mercury. Two engines, scale copies of main line engines, were to be used and these were kept at the Mercury for many years. Permission to build such a line was refused.

Another non-starter was a projected line from Bishop's Waltham to Bursledon, with a possible extension to Hamble.

The railway line to Shell-Mex, officially known as Hamble Road Sidings, was opened in 1917, being built for the No. 1 Southern Marine Acceptance Depot and for Avro who, the previous year, had bought several of the fields which now make up the aerodrome. The line was sold to Shell-Mex in 1921 but was bought back by Avro in 1923.

In 1903 the Parish Council asked the London & South Western Railway to provide a halt at the arch in Hamble Lane but this was refused and Hamble had to wait until January 1942 before Hamble Halt was opened for the convenience of those working at Hamble's aircraft factories and to save petrol from being used in private cars.

Had the proposed railway come to Hamble Village, the story might have been different. The River might well have become too commercialized, the whole tempo changed and the recreational centre it is today might never have materialized.

Transport

The villagers had little need to travel and, for the most part, stayed in Hamble although there were horse brakes and other carts available. The gentry had their own horses and carriages and were independent.

Phipps' GMC 30 cwt. bus on the Hamble-Netley-Woolston route.

By 1859 John Saunders was in business as a carrier and ran a daily omnibus to and from Woolston. William Hooker, of the Victory Inn, took on the job of carrier in 1887 and continued for many years. Carriages and flies could be hired there as well as at the Bugle Inn.

The motor, however, was on its way and a photograph taken in the grounds of The Cottage shows Admiral Fullerton and his friends with their conveyances in 1903. These vehicles were:

   (1)   A Rex 3 h.p. motor cycle with side carriage, 1902-3.
   (2)   c. 1899-1900 Werner ¾ h.p. motor cycle.
   (3)   1902 Werner motor cycle.
   (4)   A mid-1903 De Dion Bouton 8 h.p. single cylinder car.
   (5)   1903 2¼ or 2½ h.p. Ormonde motor cycle, with trailer.

A regular brake service which had run between Hamble and Netley was abandoned in 1902 and there were other occasions when there was no 'bus service to Woolston or even Netley Station. Eventually, however, Mr. Phipps of Netley acquired a motor 'bus which provided a regular service until bought out by the Hants & Dorset Bus Company in 1926. His 'bus had canvas curtains to keep some of the rain out and the local humorists crowded to the back to try to lift the front wheels off the ground!

Aircraft

It is reported that a 'fire balloon' took off from Hamble Marsh, to the amazement of the locals, in May 1786, rose to a great height and headed for Portsmouth. This was probably Hamble's first sally into the realms of aeronautics. In those days

the method was to light a fire of straw and chopped wool beneath the aperture but it was not then understood why hot air caused the balloon to rise.

It was not until 1911 that the village became involved in heavier-than-air machines.

Those who have mastered the art of building ships in wood, who can use an adze to give a vessel fair lines and who can get the bevels right and watertight and steam the ribs of small craft can turn their hands to almost any job and need have little fear of unemployment.

So it was that, when Lukes, the boatbuilders at the mouth of the River, had need of more work, they occupied themselves building aircraft. This started in a small way about 1911. Hamble River Luke Co., with the two Luke brothers as directors, was joined by Mr. E. Bircham, an engineer, and Mr. F. Murphy, a designer, and the H.L.1 was born. It was exhibited at the 1914 Olympia Aero Show. It was a two-seater powered by a 150 h.p. engine with a maximum speed of 65 mph. Although it did fly after several modifications, it was never a great success and the firm went into liquidation just before the 1914 war. The H.L.1 project was abandoned.

The two Luke brothers, however, started again early in the war, building wings, floats and other wooden components for other firms and sold part of their site to Richard Fairey who had been Works Manager for Short Brothers of Rochester.

In 1914 A.V. Roe, the first Englishman to fly (he had been flying since 1908), came to Hamble from Manchester where he had a big aircraft factory. He bought Farmer Brown's 'Big Field' which lay between Hamble Lane and Southampton Water (now occupied by Petters) and there built a factory near the roadway. The flying field had a gentle slope to the water.

So far as the village people were concerned, it was a most unpopular project. There was no unemployment in the village

Admiral Sir John Fullerton at The Cottage, School Lane, in a mid-1903 De Dion Bouton 8 hp single cylinder car, with friends in a Rex 3 hp motor cycle with side carriage c. 1902-3; Werner ¾ hp motor cycle c. 1899-1900; 1902 Werner motor cycle; and 1903 2¼ or 2½ hp Ormond motor cycle.

A Borel Waterplane at Hamble Point, 1911.

Avro 504 being loaded on the shore at Southampton Water with parcels and packets for delivery to Torquay in 1913. As a matter of interest Post Office Air Mail was to begin in 1936.

and inhabitants did not want their peaceful way of life disrupted. About 40 key men were imported from Manchester and the rest of the workers came in from Woolston in special 'buses. Avro built several houses in Hamble to entice workers to live near their work but there was great reluctance to come where there was no gas or main drainage.

On 2nd September 1913 the Admiralty yacht *Enchantress* lay off the mouth of the Hamble and the First Lord of the Admiralty, Mr. Winston Churchill, came ashore intent on a potential new war weapon, a Navy waterplane, the Sopwith 90 h.p. tractor biplane. Churchill was a passenger as the plane took off unsteadily and flew around Southampton Water. He subsequently took flying instruction at the same airfield.

There was considerable political in-fighting between the War Office and the Admiralty concerning aircraft designs and the way in which the aircraft industry should be organized. No agreement was reached and, in June 1914, the Royal Naval Air Service was formed. This was good news for Hamble for it meant that contracts might come to local builders which would have been most unlikely if everything had been left to the Royal Aircraft Factory at Farnborough.

In spite of labour difficulties, production went ahead, for the war made great demands. A slipway was built for seaplanes and flying boats. The factory had its own design office and soon seaplanes were being produced for the newly-formed Royal Naval Air Service. With a labour force of 500 men and women, the factory was eventually to produce Avro 504's at the rate of seven planes a week.

Both Fairey and Roe were intent on developing seaplanes. Fairey, in partnership with George Parnell Company and Bristol and Westland Aircraft of Yeovil, was testing 'Short' type seaplanes fitted with 150 h.p. engines and employing about 70 people of whom 15 were women trained for fabric and light metal work. Much experimental work was carried out at the beginning of the war and, after tests, orders were received for 100 'Hamble Babies', biplanes with floats fitted with 130 h.p. Cleigit engines. These were used extensively during the war. This was joined in 1917 by a larger Fairey design, the 'Compania', which was intended for use with a Cunard ship of that name converted into an aircraft carrier. By the end of the war, about 200 were employed at Faireys.

Towards the end of the war, large hangars were being built in Hamble on a site now occupied by Shell-Mex & B.P. These were to house flying boats and seaplanes. Some 400 R.A.F. and R.N.A.S. personnel of the newly-formed No. 1 Southern Marine Acceptance Depot were accommodated in buildings erected by P.O.Ws north of the roadway. As it happened, the war came to an end and the project was abandoned, leaving the buildings roofless. The high walls were demolished on the arrival of Shell-Mex in 1921.

Inevitably the end of the war brought a slump in the aircraft industry. Luke Bros. closed down and moved upriver, reverting to their first love, boat-building. Faireys decided not to go into civil flying but drastically reduced their work force and continued to develop military planes. Among the types developed were the 3F, 3P, Seal, Fairey, Sea Fox, Fly Catcher, Fairey Fox, Battle and Swordfish – the last a torpedo-carrying plane. Avro, on the other hand, aimed for the civil market, developing the 504 type of land planes and seaplanes.

At Easter 1919, three 504s at Hamble gave joy-rides at £1 a trip to 359 passengers but the slump came and expansion was impossible. Between 1919 and 1930, over 300 504s were built, as well as several less successful designs, such as the Avro Triplane, the Avenger, the Bison and the Ava, the largest plane of its day. The Avro Avian, a light 30 h.p. plane, was a success, however,

and the Hamble Works Test pilot, Bert Hinkler, flew solo to his native Australia in 15½ days in 1928.

Avro was also building auto-giros to Juan de la Cierva's design and these forerunners of the helicopter were watched with due interest by the village. To start the early models a rope was wound round the upright shaft of the rotor and about twenty of the local lads would run away to give the blades a start, all falling flat when the rope came clear. There was no shortage of volunteers. Once, much to A.V. Roe's consternation, Cierva insisted on flying the contraption into the hangar.

Cierva was killed in a flying accident in Spain in 1938 when on the verge of successfully powering the rotor.

It was not until after the First World War that some of the fields of wheat, barley and meadow were taken over to form a small airfield where the present one is situated. It was then by no

Avro Ava. Largest plane of her day, on her maiden flight at Hamble, 1924.

Bert Hinkler (centre) and the plane in which he flew to Australia. Roy Chadwick is on the left and Mr. R.J. Parrot, General Manager of A.V. Roe, is on the right.

Juan de la Cierva and his Autogiro, c. 1930.

Autogiros outside Avro's factory, 1931.

means as extensive as it is today. Here the Hampshire Aero Club operated until 1933 when it moved to Eastleigh.

J.D. Siddeley, founder of Armstrong-Siddeley Ltd. and later Lord Kenilworth, foresaw the development of civil aviation and the need for highly-trained personnel. To cater for this eventuality, Air Service Training Ltd. was founded at Hamble in June 1931, with Group-Captain R.J.F. Barton, C.B.E., in charge. The School incorporated the aircraft, pilots and staff of the R.A.F. Reserve of Officers Training School from Coventry and was opened by H.R.H. the Duke of Gloucester.

Hamble was chosen because it offered facilities for both land and sea planes. Every flying instructor had to hold an R.A.F. Flying Instructor's A1 Certificate. The Company offered advanced flying training to British, Dominion and foreign students and to R.A.F. personnel, and the airfield to the west of Satchell Lane was enlarged.

Air Service Training at one time had over 400 students in their Radio, Navigation, Flying and Engineering Schools and men of 33 different nationalities included German and Japanese pilots who later fought against this country.

By 1934 business had improved and A.S.T. and Armstrong-Whitworth amalgamated. Within a couple of years, fears of another war brought Government contracts, and design work on the first 1,000-h.p. twin-engined bombers started. These were produced early in the Second World War.

The first successful trials of re-fuelling in flight were staged at Hamble in 1937. This was a brainchild of Alan Cobham who wished to be able to take off in flying boats without much fuel but with a full payload of cargo and, once airborne, take on his fuel. While at Hamble he crashed while piloting one of Cierva's early autogiros.

1938 saw the first of 14 Ensigns take the air at Hamble. These had been ordered by Imperial Airways in 1936 and were the first large four-engined all-metal transport planes. They had a wing span of 123 feet.

The Ibis, too, was another plane to make her debut at Hamble. She had been designed and built at Thornhill and was a flying boat with wheels.

Between 1939 and 1945, the factory was used extensively for salvage and repair work and about 2,000 Spitfires and Hurricanes were put back into service. A fighter damaged in battle but still flyable would inform his Flight-Commander that he was 'going home to mother' – mother being Hamble. He would then land at Hamble, where his aircraft was inspected, repaired and re-armed and, in a matter of hours, would take off and rejoin his squadron. There was much cannibalization and machines which required major repairs or even re-building would be flown to their squadrons by men and women of the Air Transport Auxiliary Service, many of whom lived in the village.

Churchill's personal York aircraft was fitted out by A.S.T. who also carried out the conversion of pilots of land planes to flying boats for Imperial Airways for their overseas routes and were pioneers in this country of the Standard Beam Approach system. A.S.T. technicians worked on this project at Watchfield, near Swindon. About 800 were employed during the war but, with peace, work fell off and the labour force was reduced to about 200 doing sub-contract work. This, however, was not sufficient to keep going and in 1959 the factory was taken over by Petters for the production of refrigerators and compressors.

In 1936, the British Marine Aircraft Co. was formed to build the Sikorski 542 commercial flying boat under licence and the Earl of Hardwicke's estate was bought. A factory, slipway and housing estate were built but no planes. The company was reorganized by H.P. Folland, the Chief Designer of Gloster Aircraft. It became Folland Aircraft Ltd. in 1937 and was soon busy producing Blenheim and Beaufort parts.

During the war, with a labour force of over 3,000, components were made for the Spitfire, Wellington, Beaufort, Beaufighter, Buckingham, Sunderland Flying Boat, Mosquito and Hornet. When peace came, orders dwindled and it was a struggle to keep a labour force reduced to 1,800 fully occupied on any type of production available.

In 1950 Mr. W.E.W. Petter joined Follands and four years later became Managing Director and Chief Engineer. Work in

Aerial view of Hamble from the river to Avro's factory.

these early days of the Jet Age had been centred on producing parts for the Dove, Vampire, Venom, Chipmunk, Comet, Canberra, Britannia, Hawker Hunter and Sea Vixen but Mr. Petter pioneered the development of the Gnat which was designed and built in Hamble and its successful production lasted until 1962.

Government policy in 1959 caused ten aircraft factories to form one large group and, in the merger, Follands became part of the Hawker-Siddeley Aviation Group and in April 1977 became British Aerospace, although their social and sports activities still operate under the name of Folland.

The footpath which ran from the Church across the fields and aerodrome to Hamble Lane was closed for security reasons in 1939 and was never reopened, the parish being recompensed sufficiently to buy the Recreation Ground in Hamble Lane.

Oil

By 1920 more and more ships were turning from coal to oil fuel and it was to cope with the demand for bunkering fuel that the British Tanker Co., a subsidiary of British Petroleum Ltd., moored a 5,000 ton vessel fitted with oil tanks in Southampton Water off Hamble Common.

This ship, *British Maple*, had had a strange life. She had been built by Swan Hunters at Wallsend-on-Tyne in 1898, probably for a foreign company for she was not registered in London until 1917 when she was called *Mapleleaf*. In 1912 the murderer Crippen had sailed in her for Canada and was caught by means of wireless, the first such use of the new invention.

During the First World War she had been camouflaged as a British battleship but by 1925 her name was changed back to *British Maple*. She received the bunkering fuel from larger tankers but it soon became apparent that storage for larger quantities had to be found and in 1924 B-P bought Brick Kiln Field and St. Andrew's Field adjoining Hamble Common. There they built storage tanks and a jetty.

The jetty, of course, had to cross the beach and, as there were ancient copyholders' rights to take carts along 'Tithe 150', as the stretch of shore is known, in order to collect seaweed for fertilizing their fields, a kink had to be made to give sufficient headroom for the exercise of this old right.

When the pier was built, the limits of Southampton Harbour Board finished on a line from Fawley Beacon to the shore end of the new jetty and the pierhead was therefore outside the Harbour Board's jurisdiction.

By 1932 the installation had to be extended to store more and lighter fuels and again in 1938 still more tanks were erected and storage for 24,000 tons of oil was built underground. The total storage capacity was about 330,000 tons. Further tanks were built in the old loam pit in Satchell Lane and in 1939 a pipe line was constructed connecting the installation with London Airport and the Midlands, the first of its kind in the country.

During the last war, all the fuel pumped through PLUTO (Pipe Line Under The Ocean) to the armies landing in France came through the Hamble depot. A German magnetic mine fell between the tanks during one raid but failed to explode.

Ferry

Hamble Ferry to Warsash seems to have been started as one of the manorial rights of Hamble Priory in the twelfth century on land granted by the Bishop of Winchester. It was acquired by William of Wykeham and endowed to St. Mary's College in 1391. It remained in the hands of Winchester College until the beginning of the present century when it was bought by Coopers, the brewers, who were owners of the Bugle Inn, once known as The Ferry House.

Manorial records tell that the riparian (water frontage) tenants of Titchfield, who were boat owners, were obliged to take the Abbot, Canons or members of the Lord's household and their horses free across the estuary of the Hamble when necessary. If they had to convey them up the water to Southampton, they were always to be recompensed by a repast or by 4d in money, whichever they preferred.

It is clear, then, that the Ferry in early days was capable of carrying horses and in 1598, according to the Winchester Court Rolls, 'any tenant of this manor who crosses or returns by water with his horse is to be charged a half-penny for that horse or a farthing if without a horse whatever the time of crossing'.

That year, Thomas Cooper 'took of the Lord the right of the passage of the ferry over the River Hamble with the carrying of all persons, goods and chattels whether coming or going. To be held by the said Thomas and his assigns according to the customs of the manor at the rent of five shillings a year. And he made fealty and was admitted tenant'. 'Fealty' was the obligation of fidelity on the part of a feudal tenant to his Lord. Failure to perform such feudal service was 'felony'.

The reference to 'goods and chattels' as well as persons suggests that the ferry used to be of greater dimensions and importance than the present craft. When the shipbuilder Parsons moved from Bursledon to Warsash in 1804, he noted that there was a regular and reliable ferry service from Hamble which could be used by those of his workmen living on the west side of the River.

The exact location of the early ferry is uncertain but may well have been straight across the river from the Quay although a survey map of 1797 shows it in its present position. Until 1940 the ferry had always been rowed.

Sport

Sport in Hamble in the early part of this century took the form which was common to most villages where the enthusiasts made their own pleasure. The local football team played on good turf on the Common where they marked out a pitch, put up some goal-posts, chased the cows away and cleaned up after them and uprooted any gorse bushes which encroached. The local team arrived changed for the fray, leaving the changing room (a little hut on wheels) for the convenience of the visiting team. The game itself, by modern standards, was lighthearted and lacking in finesse. Each player, of course, paid his own way and contributed to the few running expenses.

When the new factories started their own sports clubs, they had better pitches which were looked after by a groundsman, and their players were expected only to play and not to do all the odd jobs. As many of the village team worked at one or other of the factories, the better players were enticed away from the local team and it was inevitable that the village team eventually ceased to function.

Village cricket was played on fields off Hamble Lane, where The Summer House now stands, and later at what is now Flowers Close. This was also affected by the factory sports clubs and failed, but not before many matches had been played against the Training Ship Mercury which could field a team second to none, for their captain was C.B. Fry, who played cricket and football for England as well as holding the world's long jump record for many years, and his many friends liked to come to Hamble to play. Among those who played cricket on the Mercury's ground were W.G. Grace, Ranjitsinhji and his nephew Duleepsinhji, 'Plum' Warner, Maurice Tate, C.B. Fry's son Stephen (who later captained Hampshire), Phil Mead and many others who were household names in their day.

Since the Second World War, sport in Hamble has expanded enormously with various teams playing for Hawker-Siddeley, Shell-Mex, the College of Air Training and the Youth Club, while other teams play on the Recreation Ground.

The non-spectator sport of competitive sailing, however, has probably attracted a greater number of participants with several hundred racing at Hamble every weekend. Yacht racing has always been a sport in which there is no referee, each helmsman being trusted to comply with the rules or to retire from the race, his conscience proving a sufficient master of his behaviour. There is, of course, machinery for settling disputes where two competitors both think they are in the right, but protests and appeals have been far less frequent than in most other sports. This trust has acted as a training in self-discipline and, together with the custom of the sea that all vessels must render assistance to those in peril, has instilled a sense of responsibility in its adherents which must surely have affected their everyday living. The sport, which used to be for the few and during the summer months only, has expanded enormously and, since the advent of wetsuits and thermal clothing, is now a winter sport as well.

Walls

There are many interesting walls in the village but one has to delve into the past to learn their story. Geologists tell us that those who built Beaulieu Abbey brought the stone with them from the Caen district of France.

Public distrust of the Church was stirred up by Henry VIII with malicious rumours about secret passages and nefarious goings-on. These were probably largely untrue but had the effect of minimizing the outcry when the Abbeys were sacked. Some of the rumours persist to this day and stories of secret passages are common.

Stones from the sacked abbeys were used to build castles for defence, St. Andrew's among them.

Hamble Castle (St. Andrew's) eventually became derelict and the local inhabitants took the stone to build walls in the village. The retaining wall at the back of Copperhill Terrace in Well Lane is one example of what became of them. They are found, too, at the bottom of the wall behind the dinghy park but here the wall has been raised with other stones. The wharf at Quay House was also built with them.

The trading craft from Hamble often returned 'in ballast', that is, they gave her stability by loading her with boulders off the beach, and these rocks were tossed overboard on reaching Hamble and were used to build up the walls. No detailed examination has been made but it is evident that the wall includes stones from the West Country, Wales, Ireland, France, Norway – indeed, from most of the countries with which local vessels traded. There are many alien stones built into old houses in the village.

Ferry Hard and Hut, 1920.

The Ferry Hard looking towards the Quay.

High Street, 1930, showing several of Hamble's businesses at the time.

It appears that from Roman times, until Henry VIII's reign, there are no records of bricks being made in Hampshire. The earliest examples of the revived industry of brickmaking are those in the ruined foundations of St. Andrew's Castle.

Beds of clay can be found at many places locally. A field on what is now Shell-Mex was known as Kiln Field. The brickworks of Lower Swanwick were started in 1894 by Hooper & Ashby. Hooper's Cement Company became Bursledon Brickworks in 1903 and in 1960 was owned by the Sussex & Dorking Brick Co. Bricks were shipped out of the Hamble and sent to London, Christchurch and other ports.

There was a cement works at Warsash in 1864 where mud and chalk were burnt. Portland Cement was first produced in 1924. Clay was dug in many places but the good clay was eventually exhausted, leaving only that with too much iron in it for brickmaking. Gravel, too, was dug at two pits in Satchell Lane and one by the Green. There is also a considerable deposit beneath the Recreation Ground.

Shops and Businesses

In the early years of the 20th century the only shops were a sweet shop in the Square (now occupied by a yacht broker); Tom Norris's grocery (now a chandlery, Compass Point, though Norris opened originally in the first house on the north side of Lower High Street), behind which there was a small bakery run by one of the many Williamses of the parish; and the bakery next to Ye Olde Whyte Harte run since 1879 by the Hookers, another extensive local family. When the twin sons of the original Hooker retired in 1967, the bakery was taken over by the adjoining public house.

Claude Bevis opened his newsagents in the Lower High Street in 1923. (Before then the nearest newsagent was W.H. Smith's bookstall at Netley Station.) He retired in 1967 but it is still a thriving business though in 20 years it has changed hands 8 times.

Lankester & Crook, whose headquarters were in Woolston, opened a store in the Square, next to the Olde House, in 1924 and this was the main shopping centre until 1983 when it was taken over by the shopping chain Sperrings.

Before the last war, there was no bank nearer than Woolston but there are now branches of three of the Big Four and two sub post offices. The site of the first of these was in Portland Cottages (now Portland House) in Lower High Street where the postmistress also managed the small telephone exchange. Hamble was the name of the exchange for the village and for neighbouring Netley until 1982 when, to the chagrin of independent-minded parishioners, it was incorporated into Southampton.

All these were at the eastern end of the village. Later there was a shoemender in St. Andrew's Buildings, opposite the Church, and another, Cecil Lewis, who also sold shoes, next to Spake's, the Butcher (established 1921).

At the time of the coronation of George VI in 1937, a new public house, named The Coronation, was built at the western end of Hamble and a small parade of ten shops was built opposite, on Coronation Parade. The public house was renamed The Harrier in 1970 owing to the involvement of nearby British Aerospace with production of that famous aircraft due, in 1982, to become even more renowned owing to the Falklands conflict. (The Hamble factory produces the fuselage, canopy, fin and tailplane for the Harrier. In 1981 the Ground Trainer was

Village smithy (now Lloyds Bank), in High Street.

replaced by the Hawk, designed, like the Harrier, at Kingston and now sold worldwide for RAF training.)

There are few articles which cannot be obtained in the village (except, perhaps, walking shoes as opposed to yachting footwear) but unfortunately many newcomers prefer to travel to the City of Southampton or to large supermarkets. Satchell Stores, a family concern, flourished for many years in Daffodil Terrace.

As for business concerns, a few years ago there were more than 90 in the village, ranging from giants like Rank Marine (owners of two of the marinas) to thriving one-man concerns.

Walker Wingsail Systems PLC, a small firm which started in 1981, took premises on the disused airfield and, by 1987, had received orders for two of their revolutionary fuel-saving devices. These were installed in two ships, the cargo ship *Ashington* and the chemical-carrying *Orionman*.

As in most other small places, roads were not built for heavy traffic and, although Hamble is not on the way to anywhere else, it nevertheless receives more than its share owing mainly to its popularity as a yachting centre and, secondly, to the number of industrial premises, unusual in small communities.

Perhaps the greatest change noticeable at the older end of the village has come about through the construction of marinas: first at Port Hamble (originally Luke Bros.), followed upriver by Mercury, then downriver by Hamble Point on the site of Fairey Marine and now known as Hamble Point Marina. Before the advent of these very 20th century 'necessities', yacht owners sank their own improvised moorings in the happily uncluttered river

The Baker's van delivering in Netley.

and rowed ashore in their tenders. Dinghies were merely pulled up above high water mark. Now it costs the owner of quite a small yacht at least £1,000 a year to moor her in a marina, more than £19 to park his dinghy in the Parish pound, while the waiting list for river moorings is at least ten years long. Such is the price of Hamble's popularity.

Cricket in the High Street, outside Norris's Grocery.

Village Activities

Besides the social and sports activities connected with the big concerns, practically every aspect of life is catered for in the village.

Hamble Players have produced plays for more than a quarter of a century and have received numerous awards for their productions; the choral society formed in 1949 is now incorporated with that of Sarisbury and is very active; the Women's Institute has been very successful since 1946 and now has a flourishing Friday Market; the Churchwomen's Fellowship has a satisfactory membership as has the Sunday School; there are play schools for toddlers and children up to the age of five; while the older parishioners can attend the Hamble Club. Hamble Old Boys' Hockey Club has had an excellent reputation for many years.

In 1986 the BBC series 'Howard's Way', based on Bursledon, renamed Tarrant, attracted numbers of fans to Hamble with coach tours from London including trips up the Hamble River. Some years before, Hamble had figured in the film 'True as a Turtle' and the ITV children's serial 'Orlando'. The radio programme 'Any Questions?' has twice been broadcast from Hamble as well as Wilfred Pickles's 'Have a Go' and also 'Down Your Way'.

Plus, of course, there are the yacht and sailing clubs for which Hamble is noted worldwide.

T.S. Mercury Band marching up the High Street c. 1930.

79

A corner of the High Street, 1970.

The Future

Hamble has, over the years, undergone many changes but has been able to adapt to the altering requirements without losing its character.

Changes of occupation have been taken in their stride but now that the big houses have been demolished and their grounds developed, an overwhelming change has taken place: Sydney Lodge has succumbed to the aircraft industry; Ravenswood has been superseded by the Crowsport estate of some thirty bungalows; Hamble House made way for many smaller houses and prefabs; The Copse bulldozed and replaced by scores of more houses while the Mercury has given way to a vast estate.

This has brought into the village a large population – a population many of whom do not work locally, shop locally or take part in local activities. They merely use the village as a dormitory – and that Hamble has never been.

Villages, even with the great range of dissimilarity of their inhabitants – the wealthy, the doctor, the plumber, the farm labourer or impoverished gentry – have a bond, a community spirit, a respect for each other's ability or allowance for the other's shortcomings. Such spirit is missing in towns and large communities.

May Hamble remain a village!